MY FATHER'S FABLE

by Faith Omole

My Father's Fable premiered at the Bush Theatre, London,
on 17 June 2024.

MY FATHER'S FABLE
by Faith Omole

Cast

Roy	Gabriel Akuwudike
Favour	Rakie Ayola
Peace	Tiwa Lade
Bolu	Theo Ogundipe

The role of Father's Voice was voiced by Babaibeji (also Yoruba consultant)

Creative Team

Director	Rebekah Murrell
Associate Director	Taiwo Ava Oyebola
Set & Costume Designer	TK Hay
Lighting Designer	Simisola Majekodunmi
Sound Designer	XANA
Composer & Musical Director	Ayanna Witter-Johnson
Movement Director	Rachael Nanyonjo
Casting Director	Olissa Rogers CDG
Costume Supervisor	Malena Arcucci
Voice & Dialect Coach	Esi Acquaah-Harrison
Intimacy Coach	David Thackeray
Assistant LX	Luca Panetta
	Luke Goodlitt
Assistant Costume Supervisor	Ellen Rey de Castro
Production Dramatherapy	Wabriya King
Production Manager	Adam Jefferys
Company Stage Manager	Lucy Ventham
Assistant Stage Manager	Africa Blagrove
Production Electrician	Kevin James
Production Carpenter	Shaun Barber
Scenic Carpenter	John Ellis

Original recorded music features performances by

Drums, African Ancestral Rhythm Keeper	Dembis Thioung
Drums, Talking Drum	Michael Adesina
Singers	Tobi Adebajo, Gabriel Akuwudike, Rakie Ayola, Lola Brooks, Tiwa Lade, Bobbie Little, Mogali Masuku, Baker Mukasa, Rebekah Murrell, Theo Ogundipe, Faith Omole, Sule Rimi, Paul Syrstad, Ayanna Witter-Johnson

With thanks to Centre Stage Scenery for set construction services. With special thanks to Katie Greenall and Sola Olulode.

This production is generously supported by Charles Holloway.

Cast

Gabriel Akuwudike | Roy

Gabriel Akuwudike trained at Drama Centre in London.

His work in theatre includes: *Hamnet* (RSC); *King Lear* (Globe); *Blackmail* (Mercury); *Either* (Hampstead); *Time is Love* (Finborough); *Dealing With Clair* (Orange Tree); *A Gym Thing* (Small Things); *No One is an Island* (Tangle).

His work in television includes: *Screw* series 2 (STV Productions/ Channel 4); *The Doll Factory* (Buccaneer Media/Paramount+), *Lord of the Rings: The Rings of Power* (Amazon); *Hana* series 3 (NBC Universal/Amazon); *Ridley Road* (Red Productions); *War of the Worlds* series 2 (Urban Myth Films); *Cursed* (Netflix); *Game of Thrones* (HBO); *Berlin Station* season 3 (Epix); *Brexit: The Uncivil War* (House Productions/Channel 4); *The Bisexual* (Hulu/Channel 4); *The Informer* (Neal Street Productions).

His work in film includes: *The Beautiful Game* (Netflix) and *1917* (Neal Street/Amblin).

Rakie Ayola | Favour

Rakie Ayola is a producer and actress who grew up in the Ely district of Cardiff. She is recipient of a BAFTA Best Supporting Actress Award, a BAFTA Cymru Best Actress Award and the BAFTA Cymru Sian Phillips Award and the Black British Theatre Best Female Actor in a Play Award.

Her work includes: *Mom, How Did You Meet The Beatles* (Chichester Festival Theatre); *The Glow* (Royal Court); *On Bear Ridge* (Royal Court/National Theatre of Wales); *Strange Fruit* (Bush); *The Half God Of Rainfall* (Kiln); *Harry Potter and the Cursed Child* (West End).

TV and film includes includes: *Kaos, Been So Long* (Netflix); *Anthony, The Pact, Noughts & Crosses, Shetland* (BBC); *Grace* (ITV); *Alex Rider* (Amazon); *Brexit* (Channel 4).

Rakie is co-founder of Shanty Productions with her husband Adam Smethurst. She is Executive Producer on short films *Hedgehog* and *Safe Space*, feature films *Diamond Sky* and *Twelfth Night*, and BBC TV series *The Pact* (S2). Rakie is a Trustee of the Actor's Children's Trust and a Patron of the Childhood Tumour Trust.

Tiwa Lade | Peace

Tiwa Lade is a British-born Nigerian actress and writer. She attended the American Academy of Dramatic Arts in New York as well as the National Youth Theatre REP company in London.

Her most recent credits include *Hard Truths* directed by Mike Leigh due for release this year, *Indiana Jones and the Dial of Destiny* and *Tell Me Everything* for ITVX.

Theo Ogundipe | Bolu

Theo Ogundipe is an actor and musician born in Nigeria, raised in the United Kingdom, and trained at the BRIT School and Mountview.

Theatre credits include: *Cymbeline, Troilus & Cressida, King Lear, Hamlet* and *A Midsummer Night's Dream* (RSC); *Julius Caesar* (West End); *Coriolanus, Desire Under The Elms* (Sheffield Crucible); *The Girl On the Train* (Leeds Playhouse); *Rosencrantz and Guildenstern Are Dead* (Old Vic); *Twelfth Night* (Orange Tree); *Macbeth* (Royal Exchange).

Previous television credits include: *Top Boy, The Dark Crystal*

(Netflix); *Playing Nice* (ITV); *Age of Resistance*, *Wait for Me*, *Eastenders* and *Doctors* (BBC).

Film credits include: *Wait For Me; Love Without Walls*.

As a musician, Theo's music is an eclectic fusion of several genres including soul, hip-hop, indie and RnB. Theo collaborated alongside artist Brain Rays on several of his releases, which gained support from BBC Radio Introducing in the South West in 2021.

Creative Team

Faith Omole | Writer

Faith Omole recently won the prestigious Alfred Fagon Award, the leading theatre prize for Black playwrights, for her play *Kaleidoscope*. Currently, Faith is a story producer and writer on a new TV series for Angel Studios.

Faith is also an Olivier Award-nominated actor best known for the critically acclaimed Channel 4/Peacock comedy *We Are Lady Parts*, the hit stage show *Standing at the Sky's Edge* (National), and most recently Yaël Farber's critically acclaimed production of *King Lear* at the Almeida.

Rebekah Murrell | Director

Rebekah Murrell is an actor and director. She directed the premiere of Yasmin Joseph's award-winning Notting Hill Carnival play *J'Ouvert* at Theatre503 in 2019, and its 2021 West End transfer, produced by Sonia Friedman Productions.

Other work includes Yasmin Joseph's *First Winter* (The Place), a play inspired and performed by retired Caribbean nurses in Bedford whose work laid the foundations of the NHS, and *Knock Down Brixton* (Brixton House), a site-specific journey through five Brixton writers' stories of their town.

In 2023, Rebekah was selected for the inaugural cohort of Aluna Labs, a development programme for women stage directors working on screen. She is a BAFTA Connect member, and was one of the Evening Standard's Ones To Watch 2022. She received an Ian Charleson Commendation for her Juliet at the Globe, and was nominated for Best Creative West End Debut (Stage Debut Awards) and Best Production (Visionary Honours Awards) for her work on *J'ouvert*.

Taiwo Ava Oyebola | Associate Director

Taiwo Ava Oyebola is an interdisciplinary artist working across theatre, literature and arts and heritage based in London. Interrogating the world through their lived experiences centring the voices of historically overlooked communities is the thread that runs throughout their creative practice. Working intuitively, they use the poetic potential of language to explore afro-futurity, intimacy and care. Their writing has been performed at the Almeida Theatre, Theatre503 and with Talawa Theatre Company.

Directing credits include: *1961* and *The Sexiest Woman in the World* (North Wall); *Talking Stages* (Pleasance). Assistant directing credits: *Samuel Takes A Break...* (Yard); *here, here, here* (Stratford East) and *Man is Di Feast* (Camden People's Theatre).

TK Hay | Set & Costume Designer

TK is a theatre designer based in the UK.

Recent credits include: *Little Shop of Horrors* (Octagon Bolton/ Theatre by the Lake/Hull Truck/

New Wolsey); *Talawa Firsts on Tour* (Talawa); *Brenda's Got a Baby* (Nouveau Riche); *Mayflies* (York Theatre Royal); *Beginning* (Royal Exchange); *Constellations* (Stephen Joseph); *The Making of a Monster* (Wales Millennium Centre); *The Apology* (New Earth).

He was Best Designer at The Stage Debut Awards in 2022 and won the Linbury Prize in 2019. More can be found on his website: tkhay.design

Simisola Majekodunmi | Lighting Designer

Simisola Majekodunmi trained at the Royal Academy of Dramatic Arts (RADA) with a degree in Lighting Design.

Theatre credits include: *The Ballad of Hattie and James* (Kiln); *A Taste of Honey*, *Electric Rosary* (Royal Exchange); *Metamorphosis* (Frantic Assembly, UK Tour); *I, Daniel Blake* (Northern Stage/UK Tour); *Choir Boy* (Bristol Old Vic); *Es & Flo* (Wales Millennium Centre); *Sound of the Underground*, *Is God Is*, *Living Newspaper* (Royal Court); *Family Tree* (Belgrade Theatre & UK Tour); *Treason: The Musical in Concert* (Theatre Royal Dury Lane); *J'Ouvert* (Theatre503/ West End); *Starcrossed* (Wilton's Music Hall); *A Christmas Carol* (*Shakespeare North Playhouse*); *Nine Night* (Leeds Playhouse); *Human Nurture* (Sheffield); *The Wiz* (Hope Mill Theatre).

Dance credit includes: *Dark with Excessive Bright* (Royal Opera House); *Traplord* (180 Studios); *The UK Drill Project* (Barbican); *Born to Exist* (Netherlands and UK Tour); *AZARA - Just Another Day & Night* (The Place); *Puck's Shadow* (Watford Palace).

XANA | Sound Designer

XANA is a composer, spatial sound artist, music supervisor and a haptic specialist sound designer developing accessible audio systems for live art spaces. XANA is the music science and technology lead and project mentor supporting artists and inventors at audio research label Inventing Waves.

Theatre credits: *Dead Girls Rising* (Silent Uproar, UK Tour); *The Real Ones*, *My Father's Fable*, *Shifters*, *Elephant*, *Sleepova*, *The P Word*, *Strange Fruit* (Bush); *The Architect* (ATC/GDIF); *Beautiful Thing* (Stratford East); *Imposter 22*, *Word-Play*, *Living Newspaper #4* (Royal Court); *Rumble In the Jungle* (Rematch:Live); *Anna Karerina* (Edinburgh Lyceum, Bristol Old Vic); *The Trials*, *Marys Seacole* (Donmar Warehouse); *Earthworks*, *Sundown Kiki: Reloaded*, *The Collaboration*, *Sundown Kiki*, *Changing Destiny*, *Fairview*, *Ivan and the Dogs* (Young Vic); *Best Fit*, *...cake* (Theatre Peckham); *Who Killed My Father* (Tron); *as british as a watermelon* (Contact); *Hyde and Seek* (Guildhall); *Burgerz* (Hackney Showroom); *King Troll [The Fawn]* (New Diorama); *Everyday* (Deafinitely); *Black Holes* (The Place); *Hive City Legacy* (Roundhouse); *Glamrou: From Quran to Queen*, *Curious*, *Half-Breed* (Soho); *Blood Knot*, *Guards At The Taj* (Orange Tree); *Main Character Energy*, *Samuel Takes A Break...*, *SEX SEX MEN MEN* (Yard); *Everything I own*, *Is Dat Yu Yeah* (Brixton House).

Ayanna Witter-Johnson | Composer & Musical Director

Ayanna Witter-Johnson is a multi-talented singer, songwriter, pianist and cellist. She has a phenomenal mastery for seamlessly crossing the boundaries of classical, jazz, reggae, soul and R&B, to imprint her unique musical signature with her virtuosic tap, strum and bow with her cello into her sound and vibe.

An acclaimed and celebrated performer, Ayanna has collaborated with many stellar artists, including Anoushka Shankar, Nitin Sawhney, Andrea Bocelli and Jools Holland. She has also toured extensively across the UK, Europe and the US.

After graduating with a first-class degree from Trinity Laban Conservatoire of Music and Dance and the Manhattan School of Music, Ayanna participated in the London Symphony Orchestra's Panufnik Young Composers Scheme. Soon after, as Emerging Artist in Residence at London's Southbank Centre, Ayanna performed as a featured artist with Courtney Pine's Afropeans: Jazz Warriors. Later, whilst studying in the USA at New York's Manhattan School of Music, she became the only non-American to win 'Amateur Night Live at the legendary Apollo Theatre in Harlem, NYC.

As a composer, Ayanna has been commissioned by the London Symphony Orchestra, Güerzenich Orchester, Ligeti Quartet, Kronos Quartet and The Hip-Hop Shakespeare Company to name but a few. She was also selected as an arranger/orchestrator for the London Symphony Orchestra (Hugh Masekela, Belief) and the BBC Symphony Orchestra (Urban Classic).

Ayanna has released three EPs ('Truthfully', 'Black Panther' & 'Ella, Reuben & Ay') and put out her debut album 'Road Runner' in 2019, with its two subsequent singles 'Nothing Less' and 'Crossroads', via her own independent record label (Hill and Gully Records). Ayanna has worked with producers Marc Mac (4Hero), James Yarde (Terri Walker, Jamelia, Eric Benet) and recorded with featured artists, including pianist Robert Mitchell and rapper Akala.

With her January 2021 surprise-released EP 'Rise Up', Ayanna again combined reggae, classical, jazz and R&B to celebrate black culture and identity to uplift and inspire the next generation. The stunning collection of three tracks and videos featuring Akala on 'Rise Up', Cleveland Watkiss on 'Declaration Of Rights' and the 'Rise Up Riddim' have received a huge amount of critical acclaim.

Her TV credits include BBC One, London Live, Channel 4 (*Sing It Loud: Black and Proud*), BBC Proms and a stunning performance on *Later...with Jools Holland* (BBC One).

Rachael Nanyonjo | Movement Director

Rachael Nanyonjo is a movement director and choreographer. Rachael's training includes BA Honours in Dance Studies (Roehampton University) and MA in Choreography (Middlesex University).

Choreography & Movement Direction credits include: *Misty* (West End/New York); *The P Word* (Olivier Award), *Babylon*; *Beyond Borders* (Bush); *The Tempest* (Globe); *The White Card* (Northern Stage & UK tour); *Purple Snowflakes & Titty Wanks* (Abbey/Royal Court); *Trouble In Mind* (National); *Love Reign*, *Changing Destiny*, *In A Word*, *American Dream* (Young Vic); *The Death of a Black Man*, *Either* (Hampstead); *Pigeon English* (Bristol School of Acting); *Cinderella* (Nottingham Playhouse); *Cbeebies* (BBC); *Spine* (UK Tour); *Great Expectations*, *After It Rains* (National Youth Theatre); *Two*

Trains Running (ETT/Royal and Derngate); *Does My Bomb Look Big In This* (Soho/Tara Arts); *Macbeth* (Orange Tree); *The Jumper Factory* (Young Vic/ Bristol Old Vic); *Sleeping Beauty* (Stratford East, nominated for the Black British Theatre Best Choreographer Award); *Shebeen* (Nottingham Playhouse & Stratford East); Bernstein's *Mass* (Royal Festival Hall); *Twilight* (Gate); *The Divide* and *Cover My Tracks* (Old Vic).

Directing credits include: *Recognition* (Talawa); *Next Please!* (Almeida); *Recognition* (audio play with 45North Ltd/ Ellie Keel Productions); *Bobsleigh* (Old Vic Monologues); *Amazina* (Film); *An Alternative Musical* (National, for NT Learning as co-director); *Assata – She Who Struggles* (Young Vic, for Young Vic fresh direction); *2:1* (Kanzaze Dance Theatre at Rich Mix). As associate director: Disney's *Newsies* (Troubador); *Moonlight, Night School* (Harold Pinter/ Jamie Lloyd Company).

Choreographer screen credits include: *The Statistical Probability of Love at First Sight* (ACE Entertainment); *CBEEBIES: Christmas in Storyland* (BBC); and *Pirates* (Hillbilly Films/BBC/ BFI).

Olissa Rogers CDG | Casting Director

Olissa Rogers is a Casting Director working on a freelance basis. She began working in the industry back in Germany in 2008. She worked there until 2016 mainly on TV Series. In 2016 she met casting director, Jeremy Zimmermann, and went to be casting assistant for him on several films until 2018. She then moved on to become casting assistant to Kharmel Cochrane for commercials

and TV/Film projects. In March 2019 Olissa was approached by Theo Park and was working on big TV projects as her associate until October 2019, on projects including *Ted Lasso*. From November 2019 until February 2020 Olissa was one of the casting associates to Amy Hubbard. Olissa has also worked for Fiona Weir as one of her associates from June 2020 to April 2022.

Malena Arcucci | Costume Supervisor

Malena Arcucci is a theatre designer and costume supervisor based in London. She is co-artistic director of Mariana Malena Theatre Company.

Design credits include: *Strangers Like Me* (NT Connect/ Hackney Shed); *The Bit Players* (Southwark); *Friday Night Love Poem* (Zoo Venues Edinburgh); *Point of No Return* (Actor's Centre); *La Llorona* (Dance City Newcastle); *The Two of Us* (Theatre Deli); *Playing Latinx* (Camden's People's Theatre) and various productions in Buenos Aires, Argentina.

Associate Designer credits include: *Dear Elizabeth* (Gate); *Chiaroscuro* (Bush); *Thebes Land* and *Tamburlaine* (Arcola).

Costume Supervisor credits include: *Samuel Takes a Break...* (Yard); *Shifters, House of Ife, August in England* (Bush) *Sucker Punch* (Queen's Theatre); *Bootycandy* (Gate); *Super High Resolution* (Soho); *The Boys are Kissing, Moreno, Milk and Gall* (Theatre503); *Blues for an Alabama Sky* (as Assistant, National); *The Cherry Orchard* (Yard/HOME); *Chasing Hares* (Young Vic); *Lotus Beauty, Raya* (Hampstead).

Esi Acquaah-Harrison | Voice & Dialect Coach

Esi trained at Royal Central School of Speech and Drama in London, UK where she achieved a MA in Voice Studies.

Theatre work as a voice and dialect coach includes: *The House of Shades*, featuring Anne-Marie Duff (Almeida); *Morinho* (Theatre503); *Days of Significance, THIRTEEN* (both Arts Ed); *The High Table* (Bush); Benedict Lombe's award-winning *Lava* (Bush); *Punk Rock* (Stratford East); *Start* (Mountview); *Desert Boy*, *Love and Money* (LAMDA); *Pigeon English* (Bristol School of Acting); *Stop Kiss* (RADA); *The Importance of being Ernest* (English Touring Theatre); *Nine Night* (Leeds Playhouse); *All Roads, Beneatha's Place* (Young Vic); *Samuel Takes a Break...* (Yard); *No More Mr Nice Guy* (Broadway, Catford). On television: *Sex Education* Series 3 (Netflix).

Esi's stage experience as a singer-performer includes an exciting ten-year world tour with the world famous Cirque du Soleil show, *Totem*, in which she was the lead female singer and original cast member. This was preceded by two-years as Rafiki in Disney's *The Legend of the Lion King* at Disneyland Resort, Paris. Other singing and stage experiences include work with Luther Vandross, classical singer Jessye Norman, Michael Ball, Mariah Carey and Sir Tom Jones among many others. She is a former member of UK's London Community Gospel Choir. She sings as Diva Aretha Franklin in the UK Ultimate Divas tribute ensemble to Diana Ross, Aretha Franklin, Whitney Houston and Tina Turner. She made her West End debut as a singer in Derren Brown's top selling West End show *SHOWMAN*, and more recently appeared at the Borlase Theatre in Marlow.

David Thackeray | Intimacy Coach

David trained as an actor for five years, graduating from The Royal Central School of Speech and Drama with a degree in BA Acting - Collaborative Devised Theatre, which was a creative partnership with international touring theatre company Complicité.

Following his graduation, David transitioned into directing for stage. One of his productions garnered enough acclaim to be transferred to London's West End. Subsequently, he expanded his repertoire to include film and television, and he served as a Director and Producer for an episode of Amazon Prime's *Silent Eye*.

In 2017, David ventured into Intimacy Coordination, a field still in its infancy in the UK at the time. He became one of the first Intimacy Coordinators in the UK, integrating his expertise into the film and television industry following extensive workshops and training. David also frequently works with drama schools to impart his knowledge of intimacy guidelines to acting students and core staff, equipping them with best practices for their careers. Since then, he has contributed to an array of productions across various platforms, including Netflix, Disney, HBO, BBC, and Sky.

Wabriya King | Production Dramatherapy

Wabriya King is the Associate Dramatherapist at the Bush Theatre. Wabriya's practice is to create a space and a format to hold people safely while they navigate their experiences in relation to the theatre's work. Wabriya has previously worked on productions at Soho Theatre, Theatre Royal Stratford East, Hampstead Theatre, Royal Court, National Theatre and Paines Plough.

Credits for the Bush include: *Shifters*; *Paradise Now!*; *The P Word*; *House of Ife*; *Red Pitch*; *Overflow*; *Lava*; *The High Table*.

Adam Jefferys | Production Manager

Adam Jefferys is a Lighting Designer and Production Manager from Essex. Previously, he was the Technical Manager of the New Diorama Theatre.

Recent Work: *The Bleeding Tree*, *Under The Kundè Tree* (Southwark); *The Great Privation* (Theatre503); *The Olive Boy* (UK Tour); *Murder In The Dark* (UK Tour); *Elephant* (Bush); *It Is I*, *Seagull* (UK Tour); *Soon*, *Pilot* (Summerhall); *Philosophy of The World* (Cambridge Junction); *After The Act*, *War & Culture* (New Diorama); *Project Dictator* (New Diorama & Edinburgh); *Jekyll and Hyde* (Derby); *Everything Has Changed* (Tour & Edinburgh); *Dorian* (Reading Rep).

For more of Adam's work please visit his website: adamjefferys. com

Lucy Ventham | Company Stage Manager

Lucy Ventham originally studied Drama and Literature at the University of Essex before moving into stage management. Now based in London, she primarily works on new writing.

She has worked on a variety of productions, including West End, UK wide touring, outdoor promenade and immersive sensory theatre. Most recent credits include: *Whodunnit [Unrehearsed] 3* (Park); *Wow! Said the Owl* (Little Angel/UK Tour); *Pied Piper* (Battersea Arts Centre Beatbox Academy); *On the Beach* (Spare Tyre). Theatre credits for Bush Theatre include: *Sleepova*.

Africa Blagrove | Assistant Stage Manager

Africa Blagrove is an Assistant stage manager.

She started her Stage Management journey towards her last year of college when she applied for a stage management work placement with *Get Up! Stand Up! The Bob Marley Musical*.

Early last year, Africa joined the RADA Youth company on the technical theatre pathway where she gained skills in all technical aspects and was the Stage Manager/Head of Props for *Alice in Wonderland* which was put on at RADA with the Young Company Acting pathway.

Her ASM credits include: *Samuel Take a Break...* (Yard); *#Blackis...* (New Diorama); *Get Up! Stand Up! The Bob Marley Musical* (Lyric Theatre).

Bush Theatre

We make theatre for London. Now.

For over 50 years the Bush Theatre has been a world-famous home for new plays and an internationally renowned champion of playwrights.

Combining ambitious artistic programming with meaningful community engagement work and industry leading talent development schemes, the Bush Theatre champions and supports unheard voices to develop the artists and audiences of the future.

Since opening in 1972 the Bush has produced more than 500 ground-breaking premieres of new plays, developing an enviable reputation for its acclaimed productions nationally and internationally.

They have nurtured the careers of writers including James Graham, Lucy Kirkwood, Temi Wilkey, Jonathan Harvey and Jack Thorne. Recent successes include Tyrell Williams' *Red Pitch*, Benedict Lombe's *Lava*, and Arinzé Kene's *Misty*. The Bush has won over 100 awards including the Olivier Award for Outstanding Achievement in Affliate Theatre for the past four years for Richard Gadd's *Baby Reindeer*, Igor Memic's *Old Bridge*, Waleed Akhtar's *The P Word* and Matilda Feyiṣayọ Ibini's *Sleepova*.

Located in the renovated old library on Uxbridge Road in the heart of Shepherd's Bush, the Bush Theatre continues to create a space where all communities can be part of its future and call the theatre home.

'The place to go for ground-breaking work as diverse as its audiences' EVENING STANDARD

bushtheatre.co.uk
@bushtheatre

Supported by
**ARTS COUNCIL
ENGLAND**

Bush Theatre

Bush Theatre, 7 Uxbridge Road, London W12 8LJ
Box Office: 020 8743 5050 | Administration: 020 8743 3584
Email: info@bushtheatre.co.uk | bushtheatre.co.uk

Alternative Theatre Company Ltd
The Bush Theatre is a Registered Charity
and a company limited by guarantee.
Registered in England no. 1221968 Charity no. 270080

THANK YOU

Our supporters make our work possible. Together, we're evolving the canon and creating a bolder, more diverse, and representative future for British theatre. We're so grateful to you all.

MAJOR DONORS

Charles Holloway
Jim & Michelle Gibson
Georgia Oetker
Cathy & Tim Score
Susie Simkins
Jack Thorne
Gianni & Michael Alen-Buckley

SHOOTING STARS

Jim & Michelle Gibson
Cathy & Tim Score
Susie Simkins

LONE STARS

Jax & Julian Bull
Clyde Cooper
Charles Holloway
Adam Kenwright
Anthony Marraccino & Mariela Manso
Jim Marshall
Georgia Oetker

HANDFUL OF STARS

Charlie Bigham
Judy Bollinger
Sue Fletcher
Elizabeth Jack
Simon & Katherine Johnson
Joanna Kennedy
Garry & Lorna Lawrence
Vivienne Lukey
Aditya Mittal
Sam & Jim Murgatroyd
Mark & Anne Paterson
Martha Plimpton
Nick & Annie Reid
Bhagat Sharma
Joe Tinston & Amelia Knot
Dame Emma Thompson

RISING STARS

Elizabeth Beebe
Martin Blackburn
David Brooks
Catharine Browne
Anthony Chantry
Lauren Clancy
Richard & Sarah Clarke
Caroline Clasen
Susan Cuff
Matthew Cushen
Anne-Hélène & Rafaël Biosse Duplan
Austin Erwin
Kim Evans
Mimi Findlay
Jack Gordon
Hugh & Sarah Grootenhuis
Thea Guest
Sarah Harrison
Uzma Hasan
Ann Joseph
Lesley Hill & Russ Shaw
Davina & Malcolm Judelson
Mike Lewis
Lynette Linton
Michael McCoy
Judy Mellor
Caro Millington
Rajiv Nathwani
Yoana Nenova
Kate Pakenham
Stephen Pidcock
Miguel & Valeri Ramos Handal
Karen & John Seal
James St. Ville KC
Jan Topham
Kit & Anthony van Tulleken
Evanna White
Ben Yeoh

CORPORATE SPONSORS

Biznography
Casting Pictures Ltd.
Nick Hern Books
S&P Global
The Agency
Wychwood Media

TRUSTS & FOUNDATIONS

Backstage Trust
Buffini Chao Foundation
Christina Smith Foundation
Daisy Trust
Esmée Fairbairn Foundation
The Foyle Foundation
Garfield Weston Foundation
Garrick Charitable Trust
Hammersmith United Charities
The Harold Hyam Wingate Foundation
Jerwood Foundation
Martin Bowley Charitable Trust
Noël Coward Foundation
The Thistle Trust
The Weinstock Fund

And all the donors who wish to remain anonymous.

Supported by
ARTS COUNCIL ENGLAND

If you are interested in finding out how to be involved, please visit **bushtheatre.co.uk/support-us** email **development@bushtheatre.co.uk** or call **020 8743 3584**.

MY FATHER'S FABLE

Faith Omole

For Adebiyi, Adunola, Adebiyi Jr, Taiwo and Kehinde.

Characters

PEACE, *Black woman, late twenties/early thirties*
ROY, *mixed-heritage man, mid/late twenties*
FAVOUR, *Black woman, Nigerian accent, mid-fifties*
BOLU, *Black man, Nigerian accent, early thirties*
VOICE/FATHER, *Black man, Nigerian accent, late fifties*

Notes

The play is imagined to take place in one location, the downstairs of Roy and Peace's home, in an open-plan living area.

Words in square brackets [ ] are not spoken.

A forward-slash (/) indicates an overlap.

Characters will at various moments speak in Yoruba, the language of a tribe in Nigeria. Everything the audience needs to understand, they will. A glossary is included at the end of the script.

This text went to press before the end of rehearsals and so may differ slightly from the play as performed.

ACT ONE

Scene One

Saturday.

Quiet. An African drum is hit. The sound rings out.

VOICE. Okay okay okay.

The drum is beaten again.

Are you listening? You must listen.

*The drum is beaten again and again, till it finds its rhythm –
slow and strong. It could be a warning, it could be a call to
action.*

It is coming. Don't you see? It is coming. *Iyawo mi.* It cannot
be stopped now.

Blackout.

(*Whispered.*) Look. Look. *Wo!*

Lights up on the open-plan living area.

In the kitchen area is PEACE *standing by a large cooking
pot on the stove, and* ROY, *on the living-room sofa, working
on his laptop.* PEACE *checks inside the large stockpot and
grimaces.* ROY *looks over at her, a bemused smile on his
face.*

PEACE *takes a spoon and tastes what she has made…
she grimaces again. She looks at* ROY. *He looks away,
now typing enthusiastically and making a point of looking
focused.*

Note: This dialogue moves fast.

PEACE. Babe.

ROY. Hm?

PEACE. Babe.

ROY. Yes?

PEACE. Can you taste this?

ROY. Sorry?

PEACE. Can you taste this rice please – ?

ROY. The what, rice? Yeah sure.

> ROY *tries to steal extra time at his laptop. Beat.*

PEACE. Can you taste it now Roy?

ROY. I'm up and I'm tasting.

PEACE. Thank you.

> PEACE *looks eager as* ROY *lifts up a spoonful of rice… He looks terrified.*

ROY. Should probably blow it first, 'cause of the –

> PEACE *nods.*

> ROY *tastes the rice.*

PEACE. What do you think?

ROY.…Wow.

PEACE. Is it good?

ROY. Erm yeah, no yeah, I think so.

PEACE. Does it taste like the one my Mum made?

ROY. Is it her… recipe?

PEACE. TikTok. It's a TikTok recipe.

ROY. Right.

PEACE. Naijagirl627. Does it taste – ?

ROY. Well I can't really remember your mum's one *specifically*, but I think… it's a bit different.

PEACE. How do you mean?

ROY. Well it tastes more like a Nigerian risotto.

PEACE. A Nigerian risotto?

ROY. Yeah it's like what jollof rice *can* be, but like... mushier?

PEACE. Oh my gosh.

ROY. It's still special in its / own very different way, it's –

PEACE. / Oh my gosh, no *no* –

ROY. Peace, is there cheese in this?

PEACE. This is going to be so embarrassing!

PEACE *goes to grab the pot.*

ROY. What are you doing?

PEACE. I'm chucking it.

ROY. No Peace you're not chucking it, you've been cooking it
for nearly two hours – that's probably why it's gone creamy –

PEACE. HELP ME!

ROY. Right, okay let's – let's just... okay – We can have
something else. Pizza? I wouldn't mind a pizza?

PEACE. No, I don't want a pi– no.

ROY. There's a place that delivers African food, it's quite close?

PEACE. It has to be Nigerian food.

ROY. That's what I meant –

PEACE. You're just – You're not helping.

ROY. Stay with me babe. Okay so it's not quite rice any more.
But let it go *cold* and it's a similar texture to hummus so –

PEACE. *Hummus*, Roy –

ROY. Maybe we get a crusty loaf, some carrot sticks and make
it a Nigerian dip –

PEACE. No jokes. We're not laughing at this.

But PEACE *is now laughing.*

ROY. Or we blend it up and we make it a Nigerian gazpacho.

PEACE. ROY! Is it really that bad?

ROY*'s face says it all.*

(*With dread.*) I need to call my mum, don't I? Should I just call her?

ROY. Definitely not.

PEACE. I'm getting all flappy. I'm flapping.

ROY. Hey, *hey* – Come here.

PEACE. I need to call my – where's my phone?

ROY. Don't know –

PEACE. It's gone babe.

ROY. No it hasn't.

PEACE. I've lost it.

ROY. Did you have it when you were cleaning the spare room?

PEACE. Yes.

ROY. Did you leave it in there?

PEACE. Yes.

ROY. Okay so…?

PEACE *nods. Pause.* PEACE *looks at the pot of rice, then at the room, then at* ROY*, before looking at the pot again.*

Would you like me to get your phone for you Peace?

PEACE. Yes please – thank you – yes.

ROY *exits.* PEACE *tries to take a calming breath. She opens a window and breathes in and out then turns back to the room. She looks at the photo albums laid out on the dining table.*

Do you think I should put away all the pictures?

There is no response.

Roy?

ROY (*from off*). Can't hear you properly.

Slight pause.

PEACE. Do you think I should just hide all the pictures?!

ROY (*from off*). I can't hear you, Peace.

PEACE. Okay!

Pause. Then –

It's just I don't want him to think I'm rubbing his face in it – having all these family photos and memories. I don't want to be insensitive to –

ROY *enters with* PEACE*'s phone.*

ROY. You've got seven missed calls from your mum.

PEACE. Crap. Thank you. Thank you – Crap – Shit.

So what do you think?

ROY. About what?

PEACE. The photos, Roy.

ROY. The – ?

PEACE. Should I hide some of them?

ROY. What, the ones with your dad? No, don't think so. No.

PEACE. Really?

ROY. Well if you want to, but you don't have to. He knows you grew up with your dad.

PEACE. Maybe I'll just angle them away from the door, so it's not the first thing he sees. Yeah, maybe... Seven missed calls, that's, that's – I hope she's alright.

PEACE *dials a number on her phone and presses it to her ear.* ROY *leans against the countertop. He pulls* PEACE *in so he's holding her as she rambles.*

What I'll do is, I'll put half of them away and angle the other half, that way it's not like – actually no, I'll put them *all* away, I'll just – Hello? Mummy?

Something about PEACE *changes.*

Is everything okay? Sorry I missed your calls. Can you help me? I think I've messed up the – You're where? Why? No I don't mean it like that, of course you can, it's just –

PEACE *takes a deep breath. She looks at* ROY.

Babe, could you open the door please.

ROY. Why?

PEACE. Because my mum's at the door.

   Pause.

ROY. Right.

   ROY *makes his way across the room as* PEACE *quickly shoves the displayed photos/albums into various drawers.*

   FAVOUR *enters.*

FAVOUR. So you have ruined the rice?

PEACE. I don't know that it's ruined, but it might be different to the typical look and texture.

ROY. Lovely to see you, Favour.

FAVOUR. Yes.

   FAVOUR *and* PEACE *hug.* FAVOUR *then holds* PEACE's *face in her hands, smiling affectionately.* ROY *goes back to working.*

   My sweet daughter. You should have made lasagne.

PEACE (*tentative*). I wanted to make him something from our country.

FAVOUR. Then you should have followed a recipe.

PEACE. I did Mum and I asked you teach me yours and you said [*no*] – which is [*fine*] I – I need water, do you want water Mummy?

FAVOUR. Not right now no.

PEACE. Did we get erm – thingy? Do we have any –

ROY. Ice is in the bottom drawer.

PEACE. Thank you.

> PEACE *gets herself a drink.* FAVOUR *looks around the room as* PEACE *downs her glass then –*

> Mum? Why are you – why are you…? Did you stop by to bring something or…? Because remember you said last night that you wouldn't be around for today?

FAVOUR. You called me. About the rice.

PEACE. I know, but you were –

ROY. You were already at the door, Favour.

PEACE. Yeah that's –

FAVOUR. Are you not blessed my darling daughter? Let me see the food.

PEACE. I think we have to leave soo–

> FAVOUR *looks inside the cooking pot and laughs.*

FAVOUR. Peace! Simple rice you cannot cook?

ROY. Well I don't *hate* it. I mean I also don't *like* it but–

PEACE. Can you just tell me how to make it less watery. Should I add more rice or flour or somethi– ?

ROY. *Flour?* Flour… Sounds like a bad idea, no?

FAVOUR. Roy, go into my car and collect the things in the boot.

PEACE. What's in the boot – ?

FAVOUR. Rice. I'm going to cook it again.

PEACE. Oh, oh, but but –

ROY. That very kind but there's no / time, Favour.

PEACE. / Roy and I have to go to the airport soon.

FAVOUR. You hear that Roy? Go and get the rice quickly.

> FAVOUR *holds her car keys out for* ROY. ROY *looks at* PEACE.

PEACE. Maybe I should get the stuff.

ROY (*good natured*). Nope I'll do it, I can do it.

> ROY *goes to exit but stops.*

> Peace?

PEACE. Hm?

> ROY *signals for* PEACE *to move over to him, out of* FAVOUR*'s earshot.* FAVOUR *pretends she is too busy to notice.*

ROY. I thought you said she wasn't talking to you?

> PEACE *shrugs.*

> Right well if things are okay – Do you think that maybe we should tell her about… should we tell her the news?

PEACE. Now? Today? Erm no?

ROY. Because we're not doing it?

PEACE. Because there is enough happening today Roy and we should probably focus on the family stuff?

ROY. Sure sure, but you have thought –

FAVOUR. Rice!

PEACE. Babe can we talk about that in the car?

> ROY *nods. He exits.*

FAVOUR. What were you discussing?

PEACE. Nothing.

> *Pause.*

FAVOUR. I have been calling you since midday.

PEACE. Are you okay? Did you have a migraine?

FAVOUR. No migraine daughter but I did not get any sleep. You didn't call me back last night.

PEACE. After you hung up on me?

FAVOUR. Yes. You didn't call me back and today you ignore my calls, I was very upset.

PEACE. You said you wanted nothing to do with all this.

FAVOUR. But you are doing it anyway so here we are. I'm your mother, I support you.

PEACE. Thank you Mummy, and I *am* really sorry that –

FAVOUR. Even if you're making a huge mistake.

PEACE *tidies something that doesn't need to be tidied.*

You don't know that you're definitely related. You're being naive.

PEACE. I showed you the pictures.

FAVOUR. They are just pictures.

PEACE. He looks exactly like Dad.

FAVOUR. And people have said I look exactly like Naomi Campbell. It doesn't mean you can trust him in your home within weeks of finding out about him. You don't know the bastard's character.

PEACE. Mum, *please* –

FAVOUR. *What?* Is that not the technical term? He is your father's bastard son. What's wrong with bastard? Am I not allowed to call the boy a bastard when he is a bastard?

PEACE. Mum.

(*Gently.*) I know that finding out Dad had another family before us – I know it's hard. I know this is hard for you and it hurts and I'm sorry that –

FAVOUR *takes a sharp in-breath and shuts her eyes.* PEACE *stops talking.* FAVOUR *breathes out, she smiles, but* PEACE *is still worried.*

Why don't you sit down.

FAVOUR. I am fine. I am fine.

You better hide anything worth stealing daughter.

PEACE. You've already said. And we don't exactly have
heirlooms.

FAVOUR. Bank details, any valuables – Have you hidden them?

Beat. PEACE *has*.

Good.

ROY *enters. He carries a huge cooking pot with a bag
of rice inside, as well as other ingredients. He places*
FAVOUR*'s keys on a side table.*

ROY. Rice. Where should I put it?

FAVOUR *turns to* ROY.

FAVOUR. I said you should bring everything in the boot.

ROY. Do you need everything in the boot?

FAVOUR. I need what I asked for.

ROY. Right.

ROY *looks at* PEACE. PEACE *nods*. ROY *exits*.

PEACE. Mum please, don't talk to him like that –

FAVOUR *rolls her eyes*.

FAVOUR. Do you not think it is sudden? Presumptuous? For
the boy to just book a ticket and come here?

PEACE. A bit yeah but –

FAVOUR. He needs something. Probably money or an indefinite
visa.

PEACE. He's not the bad guy Mum, Dad left him –

Pause.

FAVOUR. So you are saying your father was bad?

PEACE. No, no I didn't mean / that.

FAVOUR. This is what I'm worried about. You ignore your
Mother and now you question your late father?

PEACE. I didn't mean it like that / Mum.

FAVOUR. You have invited this boy here to slander your father's memory in your own home –

PEACE. That is not what I'm doing –

FAVOUR. Yes. It is. And your father would be very disappointed.

Beat.

Peace, are you sure want to do this?

ROY *enters with the second bag – a duffel bag.*

ROY. There we are. The boot is empty.

ROY *looks at* PEACE *and* FAVOUR. *Their eyes fixed on each other.*

Everything okay?

Pause.

We have to leave now, don't we Peace? If we want to arrive on time?

PEACE. Erm…

ROY. It'll take about an hour and ten to get there so –

PEACE. It's too fast.

ROY. What?

PEACE. I think that erm maybe this is too fast actually…

ROY. Peace. He is on a plane from Nigeria.

VOICE (*whispered*). Okay. Okay. Okay. Are you listening?

The faintest echo of the drums.

FAVOUR. We can book him into a hotel for a few days. A few days is nothing. Just until we know who he is.

ROY. But we know who he is.

FAVOUR. She has the right to change her mind.

ROY. We know who he is. He's her brother.

The drums change now. A stuttering, insistent tapping. These are Bolu's drums.

VOICE. *Iyawo mi –*

FAVOUR *is momentarily distracted, then she's back, she shakes her head, seemingly to* PEACE *– 'Don't do this'.*

Look. Look. *Wo!*

Scene Two

Saturday. PEACE *enters the living area followed by* ROY. *And then* BOLU.

BOLU*'s drums stop. Between three of them they carry suitcases and backpacks.*

PEACE. So you can just put your stuff down anywhere, we'll take it up to where you're sleeping in a second.

BOLU. Thank you. Thank you both.

Beat. ROY *looks at* PEACE. *She thinks, then nods.*

ROY. Actually why don't I take some stuff up to the spare room now.

ROY *collects some luggage and crosses the space, as he passes* PEACE *he drops a quick kiss on her forehead.* ROY *exits and* PEACE *and* BOLU *are left alone.*

PEACE. Would you like a cup of tea?

BOLU. Tea – so British – brilliant.

PEACE. Yeah, yeah it is. Ha. Do you want one?

BOLU. No, I am not a fan of it, but thank you.

Awkward silence.

Some water would be nice.

PEACE. I have that!

> PEACE *goes to the kitchen. She checks the pot of jollof rice sitting on the stove and is relieved by what she finds. She fills two cups with water and returns.*

BOLU. Thank you.

> PEACE *watches* BOLU *as he drinks. He notices.*

Is there something on my face?

PEACE. No, why?

BOLU. You are staring.

PEACE. Oh! Right yeah – sorry.

> PEACE *puts her cup down and rearranges the sofa cushions.*

BOLU. You have a lovely home.

PEACE. Thank you.

BOLU. Have you lived here long?

PEACE. Erm, yes and no. It was Roy's place and I moved in, lived here for about six months. But then I accidentally left and stayed with my mum for a year because, I er slept there the night of the funeral and things kind of spiralled.

BOLU. Oh. Okay.

PEACE. It was small, by the way. The funeral. We didn't have too many people there. But if we had known about you... we would have invited you.

BOLU. I don't know that I would have come.

PEACE. Right. Of course, of course.

BOLU. Your mama, she never knew about me either?

PEACE. No. And she didn't know you were coming here till last night.

BOLU. Oh?

PEACE. I left it till the last minute to say, so that's my bad. Understandably, she's been finding it all a bit hard, so I'm just trying to be –

ROY *enters*.

ROY. Peace? Can I talk to you for a second?

PEACE *makes her way over to* ROY.

She's upstairs.

PEACE. What?

ROY. Your mum. She's upstairs, she's still here. She said she finished cooking but got a migraine, so she was on the sofa when she heard the car pull up –

PEACE. But I –

ROY. Yep.

PEACE. And she –

ROY. Yep.

PEACE *turns to* BOLU *with a smile*.

Sorry Bolu, be right back.

PEACE *exits, leaving* BOLU *and* ROY *alone*.

Bolu. England. How you finding it?

BOLU. In the three hours that I have been here? Cold. How do you find it?

ROY. Cold. *Great* football though.

BOLU. Who do you support?

ROY. Er… No one. I'm more of a film guy to be honest.

BOLU. I like films. Your favourite?

ROY. *Goodfellas*?

BOLU. *No*.

ROY. Oh you haven't seen it?

BOLU. Of course I have. It is just such a predictable choice.

ROY (*laughs*). Yours?

BOLU. *Spirited Away*.

ROY (*he's impressed*). Anime. Seriously? *Nice.*

ROY *likes* BOLU.

This is good right? You guys meeting.

BOLU. I think so.

ROY. Yeah. When Peace first told me a Nigerian guy Facebooked her saying he was her brother, all I wanted to do was ask if you were also a prince in need of a small loan.

That's not funny – Anyway, then she showed me the photo… She really struggled when her – your dad… I know the situation's messy but she's happy you're here. We both are.

BOLU *is unreadable.*

Just don't let erm… don't…

BOLU. What is it?

ROY. They can be really close. All three of them were really close, and since last year, after the – death – Peace and Favour – they've got… they can be…

BOLU. What?

ROY. Sometimes it can be difficult. Try not to be put off.

PEACE *enters, followed by* FAVOUR.

PEACE. Sorry to disappear. Bolu – this is my mum.

FAVOUR. Here he is! The wonderful boy we have heard so little about!

FAVOUR *gives* BOLU *a big hug. She is the epitome of warmth.*

BOLU. Hello Ma.

FAVOUR. Hello sweet Bolu!

BOLU. I did not know you would be joining us. Though I had hoped to see you.

FAVOUR *looks* BOLU *up and down, still smiling.*

FAVOUR. So… Interesting. Are you well?

BOLU. I am, thank you Ma, and yourself?

FAVOUR. You brought a lot of luggage.

(*To* PEACE.) He brought a lot of luggage for two weeks.

BOLU. I packed a lot of jumpers.

ROY. Fair enough.

FAVOUR. Are you hoping to stay indefinitely?

PEACE. Mum's joking.

FAVOUR. No I'm asking Bolu a question daughter. Is he hoping stay?

BOLU. Oh no Ma, not at all.

FAVOUR. Good. We are glad you are here but it's best to be on the same page.

ROY. Should we maybe –

FAVOUR. I hope you are not easily offended by my questions sweet Bolu?

BOLU. No. It is fine, perhaps I overpacked, Ma.

FAVOUR. We've all heard of the stories – people say they are coming for a week, overstay for five years and change their name to Tony Smith.

BOLU. Yes. But those people wish for another life. I like my life.

Pause. ROY *notes* PEACE*'s discomfort.*

ROY. Food smells good. Foods smells really good doesn't it Peace?

PEACE. Yeah.

ROY. Maybe it's time we / eat –

PEACE. Maybe it's time we eat. Does everyone want to wash their hands and get ready for dinner? Mum, you don't have to –

FAVOUR. I would like to stay for dinner.

PEACE. Great. Good. Good.

PEACE looks at ROY, *her eyes a little frantic.*

ROY. Bolu you can follow me and I'll show you the bathroom.

ROY and BOLU *exit.* PEACE *goes to speak but stops herself. Instead goes into the kitchen and collects dishes.* FAVOUR *sits at the head of the dining table.*

FAVOUR. My daughter.

PEACE stops. She looks over at FAVOUR.

FAVOUR. Everything I do is for you. You know that don't you?

PEACE. I know.

ROY (*from off*). Babe? Did you want me to ah – was there anything else you wanted me to / do before we come –

PEACE. You can come in!

ROY and BOLU *enter.*

Sit wherever. Won't be a moment.

BOLU takes a seat at the table across from FAVOUR. PEACE *and* ROY *prep food.*

FAVOUR. Bolu, I just want to clarify to you that you are very welcome here. It goes without saying, that you should never have been left behind in Nigeria at such a young age. I hope that today is the start of a beautiful relationship, for all of us.

BOLU. Thank you, Ma.

Note: PEACE *and* ROY *will bring rice, chicken, plantain and salad to the table.*

ROY. So Bolu – Nigeria in three words – go.

BOLU. Ah… Well it is beautiful, loud and fast.

ROY. You live in Abujah right?

BOLU. Yes, I moved to Lagos for work, but ended up coming back to be closer to my mama.

FAVOUR. Is your mama well?

BOLU. She had a few accidents, years back. It still makes her weak.

FAVOUR. Oh. I'm sorry to hear that.

BOLU nods politely. ROY looks at PEACE encouragingly.

PEACE. I'd love to see more pictures of where you grew up.

BOLU. You have never been to Nigeria?

PEACE. No.

BOLU. You never wanted to see it?

PEACE. Mum and Dad always said there's not much to do there.

FAVOUR. This one – she paraphrases.

BOLU. There is lots to do there, probably too much.

Now the table is set, PEACE *and* ROY *sit. They all eat.*

ROY. Well I'd like to go to Nigeria. Been trying our whole relationship to get Peace on a plane.

BOLU looks at PEACE for an explanation.

PEACE. I don't like flying.

ROY. Because she's never done it.

PEACE. Roy goes away for work all the time so it doesn't affect him too much.

Whereas I can't – I erm – I just… I get a bit claustrophobic and I don't like heights, or dark spaces so…

BOLU studies PEACE. PEACE turns and looks at ROY.

Anyway I'm going to try and conquer it. And I've always said I'd fly for a good reason.

BOLU. You should. And maybe you could come and see me on your first trip.

PEACE. Yeah, maybe. I'd really love that actually –

FAVOUR *winces*. PEACE *looks over*.

Migraine?

FAVOUR. Yes darling. Don't mind me.

PEACE. Drink something Mum.

ROY *passes* PEACE *a jug of water. She pours* FAVOUR *a glass*.

FAVOUR. Continue.

PEACE. Erm... er –

ROY. What do you do for work Bolu?

BOLU. I'm a writer – mainly journalism, a few essays.

ROY. Very cool.

PEACE. Yeah that's... wow.

BOLU. It gives me great pleasure. Yourselves?

ROY. I work in tech.

BOLU. What do you do in tech?

ROY. I'm a business intelligence developer at a company that specializes in marketing analytics and international supply chain transparency.

Slight pause.

It's actually a lot more fun that it / sounds.

FAVOUR. Peace has a fantastic job.

PEACE. I'm a teacher.

FAVOUR. She's a teacher at a very prestigious private school.

PEACE. Mainly teach history and citizenship, do you do citizenship in Nigeria?

BOLU. By another name. And do you enjoy your job?

PEACE. Sure. Course. Most of the time. Perks are good, pay is nice. I guess it's hard at the moment because I have this student – this one student and she makes my life a living nightmare – but yeah it can be erm – anyway Mum was a nurse, and Dad was a carer.

BOLU. He was a carer here? He used to be a carpenter.

PEACE. Really. Mum is that true?

FAVOUR. He… Yes I believe he may been a carpenter. But he stopped that when he came here.

PEACE. I'm learning something new about him every day.

FAVOUR. *Peace*.

BOLU. We still have lots of the things he made in my Mama's house.

PEACE. Like what?

BOLU. A crib, tables, chairs.

PEACE. I would love to see them.

FAVOUR. More water please Peace.

BOLU. If I'm honest I often asked my Mama to throw most of it away, but she always refused.

PEACE. Dad didn't make anything for the house did he, Mum?

ROY *notices* FAVOUR.

ROY. Let me get the light.

The light dims. PEACE *lights a candle, she doesn't enjoy the dark.*

FAVOUR. Better. I don't believe he did make anything for the house my darling.

BOLU. Did he not… sorry, did he not carve the bracelet you're wearing?

PEACE. This? No, I don't think so. Mum?

FAVOUR. Not to my knowledge. Why?

BOLU. I just assumed. It is a fine bracelet. Very beautiful.

PEACE. It was Mum's but I love it so she gave it to me. Bolu can I ask... how long was my dad with you?

Beat. BOLU *seems irritated.*

BOLU. He left when I was three for England. He came back briefly when I was four and then that was it.

PEACE. He came back?

BOLU. Briefly. Then he disappeared.

PEACE. Do you remember him?

Pause. BOLU *looks at his phone.*

BOLU. Sorry, one moment. I have to get this.

BOLU *exits.*

PEACE. What do you think?

ROY. Going well.

PEACE. Mum?

FAVOUR. I think you annoyed him just now. When you were asking him about your father.

ROY. He had a phone –

FAVOUR. Which makes sense. He came here to see Buckingham palace and go to Harrods. Not be reminded of the fact he never knew your dad, daughter.

PEACE. I didn't mean to –

FAVOUR. Just, be sensitive, Peace. Try not to upset the bastard.

ROY. Is your head still hurting, Favour?

FAVOUR. A little dear. Thank you for asking.

ROY. Right.

FAVOUR. In fact I don't think... I don't think I can drive home tonight.

PEACE. That bad? Have you taken any–

ROY. I can drive you.

FAVOUR. I think I need to sleep.

PEACE. Yeah probably.

> FAVOUR *gets up*. ROY *looks at* PEACE.

PEACE. Wait Mum did you mean – do you mean here?

FAVOUR. Yes please.

PEACE. Oh, Bolu's in the spare room remember?

ROY. So I can run you home.

FAVOUR. No I don't want to be on my own when I am not feeling well.

ROY. But Favour –

FAVOUR. I just need to lie down, daughter. Is that okay? Can I rest here or not?

PEACE. Yeah – yes. You can.

FAVOUR. Thank you.

> BOLU *enters*.

BOLU. Sorry I had not spoken to my mama since landing. You are leaving, Ma?

FAVOUR. Me? No. I'll just be upstairs. Have a lovely evening daughter, Roy, and it was so nice meet you sweet Bolu.

> FAVOUR *exits*. PEACE *watches after her.*

BOLU. She is staying here too?

ROY. Apparently.

FATHER'S VOICE. In our home they say *Omi ti a mamuko ni ṣan koja wa* – it means 'The water that one is destined to drink will never flow past one.' Never. Don't forget the sayings. Don't forget – don't – don't –

> *The sound of* FAVOUR *shutting the spare-room door.*

Scene Three

Saturday. Night-time. BOLU *lies on the sofa – restless. He has a thought and listens out. Then –* BOLU *gets up and inspects the living room.* BOLU*'s drums begin. The rhythm is insistent and stuttering as he begins openings drawers and cupboards. He seems to be looking for something. An item catches his attention but before he can take it a noise is heard from upstairs. Startled,* BOLU *shuts the drawer and jumps back onto the sofa. He pretends to be asleep.*

PEACE *now enters quietly. She looks over at* BOLU *as she softly walks toward the kitchen area. She stops to study his face.* PEACE *moves closer and closer until her face is inches above him.* BOLU *opens his eyes.*

BOLU. *Yepa!*

The drums stop.

PEACE. Sorry! I –

BOLU. Odẹru ba mi!

PEACE. Sorry I just wanted a drink, I didn't mean to –

BOLU. It is / okay don't worry –

PEACE. I didn't mean to wake you.

BOLU. I wasn't sleeping, I was just closing my eyes.

PEACE. Well I didn't mean to sneak up on you.

BOLU. It is fine –

PEACE. It's just I can see him. In you. I can see Dad.

Pause.

BOLU*'s face is unreadable.*

Sorry. What... What did you just say by the way? In Nigerian before?

BOLU. In Yoruba?

PEACE. Yeah. You said '*O di eye ri yam*'

> BOLU *eyes widen as he hears her pronunciation.*

BOLU. My goodness.

> (*To* PEACE.) I said 'you scared me'.

PEACE. Oh, that makes sense. I'm sorry you have to sleep on the sofa.

BOLU. You apologise a lot. I do not mind.

PEACE. In two days you'll have one of the comfiest beds you've ever slept in.

BOLU. I do not need to – two days?

PEACE. Mum thinks she'll be better by then.

> BOLU *is again unreadable. He studies* PEACE.

BOLU. So you don't speak Yoruba.

PEACE. No.

BOLU. Or hear it?

PEACE. No. Mum and Dad never spoke it to me. I sometimes heard them speak it when they were arguing but as a rule we all only spoke English.

BOLU. Why?

PEACE. Wasn't something I needed to know.

BOLU. You did not need to know the language of your home?

PEACE. This is my home.

BOLU. You have another one.

PEACE. Yeah I guess. But most people don't – it's quite normal here not to erm… Actually, I thought maybe you could teach me how to make some Nigerian food?

BOLU. Your rice today was good.

PEACE. Oh no that was Mum's. My jollof was unfit for human consumption. We didn't really have any of it in the house, but I do remember that Dad, would sneak me – why are you looking at me like that?

BOLU. Like what?

PEACE. Like I'm letting you down.

BOLU. It is just interesting. You are missing out on so much, yet you seem to seek so little.

PEACE. Bit judgy. Thanks for the feedback.

BOLU. You are just not what I expected.

PEACE. Well, neither are you.

Beat.

BOLU. I can teach you how to make some Nigerian dishes and how to speak small small Yoruba.

PEACE. Don't worry about it. You're only here for a couple of weeks –

BOLU. I want to sister. And you are right. I can be 'judgy'.

Pause. PEACE shifts, unsure what to do next.

Would you like to sit?

PEACE smiles. She sits.

You could not sleep?

PEACE shakes her head.

It is strange? To be in the same room. Talking.

PEACE. Yeah. For weeks you were like messages and pictures and suddenly you're…

It's like before you were an idea and now you're a person. Does that – ?

BOLU. Yes it makes sense.

PEACE. Can I… know something?

BOLU. Like?

PEACE. Anything. Tell me anything about you.

BOLU *looks at* PEACE, *wrestling with a thought.*

What were you like as a kid?

BOLU. As a child? Ah… I used to kòlòlò – stammer.

PEACE. Really?

BOLU. Yes. Even into my teenage years. Mama said at first I just stopped talking all together. The neighbours in the village thought I had mental problems. When I finally did speak, I could only stammer and people thought we were cursed.

PEACE. That must have been awful.

BOLU. Yes. And for a long time I thought they were right. Time passed. Now I never take my words for granted. Eni to ba mọ ọwọ araṛẹ kó nitẹ. And old proverb I try to remember. 'If one is mindful of their image, they cannot be disgraced.' Now, you tell me something about *you* sister. Sọ nkan fun mi.

PEACE *tries to repeat the sentence.*

PEACE. *Sofa mu – Sofi mukin* – Forget it. I had an imaginary friend until I was twelve.

BOLU. Twelve? In Nigeria they would have thought we were both cursed.

They laugh.

Your friend's name?

PEACE. Bobo.

BOLU. What did they look like?

PEACE. He didn't really look like anything. Actually no, he looked like me. And he wore a bowtie sometimes.

BOLU. You were lonely. Me too.

PEACE. Ask me a question.

BOLU. Why?

PEACE. So I can ask *you* one, it's only fair. That was your first question by the way brother.

BOLU. Oh I see. How did you meet Roy?

PEACE (*she grins*). At a park. I'd go every morning to run but never actually did any running, always ended up sitting on a bench.I'm pretty sure he was pretending, he swapped feet at one point.

BOLU. I like him.

PEACE. Yeah? Yeah. He's great. Not sure… not sure I deserve him. Which isn't a fashionable thing to say I know but… We actually broke up last year after the funeral, after I chose to stay with Mum – but it was awful, and he, erm, sometimes I worry that – gosh, I'm talking so much aren't I? Sorry! Er my turn – you asked two questions so I get two.

BOLU. Two questions okay – *Bèrè nkán lọwọ mi*. It means 'ask me something'. Try it.

PEACE. Bere… No.

BOLU. Try it sister.

PEACE (*whiny*). No. I feel shy.

  BOLU *laughs*.

BOLU. Okay okay okay. Ask me your question.

PEACE. Do you erm… do you resent me? For the life I've had?

BOLU.…What would make you think that?

PEACE. I don't know. Me growing up in England, education. It's tough over there isn't it? And you said about the village. And it was just you and your mum but I've had my two parents, I got Dad didn't I and you got –

BOLU (*firm*). Peace not all Nigerians dream of living in England despite what you hear. There are Africans still in Africa doing just fine. Education-wise, I happen to be pretty smart and as far as my mother is concerned – there is no one better. Me? I like my life.

  Beat.

  What is your second question?

PEACE. Did that question annoy you?

BOLU. No. Now you have had your two.

PEACE. Are you sure?

BOLU. And that is three.

PEACE. Can I ask you another one?

BOLU. Yes.

PEACE. Does it bother you if I talk about our father?

Pause.

BOLU. I want to talk about him also. I am just not sure you will
like what I have to say.

PEACE. You're angry with him?

BOLU. I am.

Beat.

PEACE. You haven't asked how he died.

Pause.

It was a heart attack. I was there.

Pause.

Mum and I both were. We were sitting in this ridiculously
noisy restaurant waiting for food, and then he he clutched
his heart and… He had this look in his eyes, this fear, this –
And he started apologising. Saying 'sorry, sorry, sorry, I'm
so sorry'. Like he knew he was dying but he hated the fact
he was making such a scene as he did, or like there was
something that he –

Slight pause.

He got so quiet in the last few years. He just seemed to grow
sadder and sadder, and would just whisper these words to
himself that I couldn't… now I think it's because he regretted
things.

BOLU. That man, he was a –

PEACE. Don't say anything bad about him.

BOLU. Do you know you have cousins in Nigeria? Brothers
that had not heard from him in decades, while he was *here*
caring for strangers. He left you behind because he died,
sister. He left me behind because he *chose* to. How can a man
like that be good –

PEACE. I said *don't* Bolu –

BOLU. It is important. To know who we came from.

PEACE. And I do. I knew him better than you did.

Pause. Things are tense.

Is it okay if this trip is just about you and me? Please.

Beat. BOLU *nods.* PEACE *paints a smile on her face.*

Great. That's – I have the day off tomorrow. I wanted you to
take to the M&M store.

BOLU. Like… Like the rapper?

PEACE. No, like the American chocolate. It's the dumbest store
ever.

BOLU. I see.

PEACE. You'll love it.

BOLU. Is it expensive?

PEACE. Don't worry about that, I'll take care of it.

BOLU. It is just that after the – [*flight.*]

PEACE. I'll cover it.

BOLU *nods but he is dissatisfied.*

I should get to bed. Last question. How do you erm… How
do you say 'brother' in Yoruba?

BOLU. Ẹ́gbọn mi.

PEACE. Ẹ́gbọn mi. That was good wasn't it? That was good.

BOLU. It was… better than the others.

PEACE. It was fluent Yoruba, brother. Stop pretending you're
not impressed.

BOLU *is charmed, he chuckles and rolls his eyes.*

Night Bolu.

BOLU. Goodnight Peace.

PEACE *leaves and the smile of* BOLU*'s face drops.*

BOLU. Peace. Hm. A terrible name.

The living area darkens… drums.

FATHER'S VOICE. Are you listening? Afẹfẹ ko ṣee gbe. Afẹfẹ ko ṣee gbe. The wind it is impossible to carry. It is impossible to carry.

FAVOUR *enters.*

Scene Four

Wednesday morning. PEACE *and* ROY *are in the living-room area getting ready to leave for work.*

ROY. It's been five days.

PEACE. I know.

ROY. Your mum has been staying here for five days.

PEACE. It's not / ideal. But it's fine.

ROY. Bolu can't settle in, he keeps going out for walks, where's he gone? It's six forty-five in the morning?! He's stuck in this one room all the time.

PEACE. She's not feeling well. What?

ROY. I'm just gonna say it – you know she didn't just come here with rice and a cooking pot, the stuff she made me get from the boot of her car – the bag. It was slightly open. I saw things.

PEACE. What things?

ROY. Bonnet, Peace. Hair bonnet, slippers, fluffy robe, toiletries, room spray. Do you understand what I'm saying?

PEACE. When you say 'slightly' open – ?

ROY. It was premeditated, Peace. She was always going to stay.

PEACE. Well she can stay overnight –

ROY. Overnight? It's been *five* days! She's in the bath at peak bathroom-traffic hour! And do you see what she's done? She's reordered all the cushions, she's changed how we stacked the plates in the cupboards. She changed bookshelves upstairs so they're in alphabetical order.

PEACE. Isn't that just nice?

ROY. It's psychological warfare!

PEACE. *Babe.*

ROY. What I'm trying to say, is that she is being very present at a time when she doesn't need to be here. Bolu and you should have more time alone.

PEACE. Bolu hasn't said anything. Bolu doesn't mind. It's you that's getting all... flappy –

ROY. I'm not flapping.

PEACE. You are a bit, you're a bit flappy.

ROY. Peace –

PEACE. Have you seen my bracelet?

ROY. Come on babe, don't you find it strange –

PEACE. – My mum's bracelet that I wear, have you seen it?

ROY. She probably moved it.

PEACE. No she didn't, I've already asked. / Shit.

ROY. I just find it weird that –

PEACE. *Shit.*

ROY. That she can't –

PEACE. Where is / it –

ROY. – let you spend any time with your long-lost brother!
I mean it's different to when it's me, I'm used to it, sure
whatever – invade our space, take over, ignore me but –

PEACE. *Why*, why are you making this about you?! So she feels
better being here whilst I get to know Bolu, so what? You're
the one ruining it, not her!

Pause.

That came out wrong. I'm sorry.

ROY *shakes his head. He busies himself, packing his bag for
work.*

I just think you're letting before factor into… [*now*] and this
is different.

ROY *carries on getting ready.*

Roy.

ROY *stops. They look at one another.*

You're so far away.

ROY. So?

PEACE *gestures for* ROY *to move closer to her, she is
ridiculously cute. She and* ROY *meet in the middle of the
room and she holds him. It's nice. And things are fine again.*

What are you thinking?

PEACE. I'm just wondering if Bolu's bored.

ROY. You're taking him out as much as you can.

PEACE. Yeah I know, but I wish I had more time off work. I'm
so behind on lesson prep anyway. I'd rather spend days doing
fun things with him, instead of wasting my time teaching
people who don't want to listen to me.

ROY. Loudmouth in Nine-E?

PEACE. She called me a bot yesterday. She said, Miss Peace

you teach like a bot. Which doesn't sound so bad when you hear it but then she *wrote* it on the board and stuck a sign up on the door.

ROY. You remember that age: the acne and braces, the who-fancies-who, the chess tournaments. It makes you hostile.

PEACE *laughs*.

PEACE. Yeah, please make jokes, if I don't laugh I'll cry.

ROY. Can I help?

PEACE. You could take Bolu out? This weekend? That way I get to catch up and you two can get to know each other more. Have some 'boy time'.

ROY. Oh don't call it boy time, babe.

PEACE. Man time? Caveman time? Macho-macho-man time? What should I call it? A lads' night?

ROY. Never a lads' night. You don't call it anything.

PEACE. Can you?

ROY. Yeah I'd love to.

PEACE. Thank you.

ROY. And I guess erm that'll give you some quality time with Favour as well.

PEACE. I guess.

PEACE *starts looking for her mum's bracelet again*.

ROY. So is she staying with us till Bolu goes then? Like what's the plan? Because Bolu shouldn't stay on the sofa any longer, it's not fair on him.

PEACE. I know, I was gonna ask if – I was just thinking that maybe – maybe Mum shares our room with me until she gets better, then Bolu gets the spare back and –

ROY. And I have the sofa?

(*Sarcastic.*) Ah yeah, great idea babe.

PEACE. Don't worry, forget it.

ROY. Actually better idea Peace, why don't I sleep on the floor, and we let your mum rest her overnight bag on the sofa –

PEACE. I was just trying to find a –

ROY. You know the maddest thing? Is that she gave you this idea.

PEACE. No / she didn't.

ROY. Last night, before she went to bed, she said that when you were young, your dad would get annoyed at her because she'd let you sleep in the bed, so he'd go / sleep on the sofa.

PEACE. That's not the / same thing.

ROY. She speaks, you respond but you have no idea what she's saying.

PEACE. This is just – Roy please, I don't want to argue with you.

ROY. I don't want to argue with *you*.

Beat.

Can we 'not argue' about my job offer?

Beat.

No arguing, just talking. Peace you said we'd speak about it in the car, but we didn't and since then we haven't had a second alone. I need to know what you think, because my boss is pushing me for an answer.

Pause.

Shall I tell you what *I* think? I think I can see myself moving out there. I think I'd love heading up the new division and I'd be great at it. I want to go. With you.

Pause.

What do you want? What do you want Peace? You can teach there. Or not. We can try new things.

PEACE *looks at* ROY. *He is contagiously excited.*

We can try new food, and hobbies. We can make friends with strangers. You could do more. Like I know you want to. We could climb the big mountain, surf down some deserts. Jump in the river, see who can hold their breath the longest. If that's too scary – fine. We'll just look at mountains and sit by the river, whatever – I don't care. You'll be with me and I'll be with you and it'll be... Is that a smile?

PEACE. Not because – It's a big decision Roy.

ROY. They've only asked for a year.

PEACE. What if they want you for longer?

ROY. It's a great opportunity.

PEACE. We'd have to fly there.

ROY. So? That's nothing.

PEACE. It's not. For me. It's not.

ROY. Right. Are you asking me to turn it down?

PEACE. No.

ROY. Are you asking me to go without you?

PEACE. No.

ROY. I need you to make a decision babe.

PEACE. Can you give me a little more time?

ROY. Peace you've had –

PEACE. I just want a few more days to think, can you let me have that please?

Pause.

ROY. Okay. I'll ask them for another week.

Scene Five

Wednesday evening. PEACE *and* BOLU *are in the living room.* BOLU*'s belonging have been moved upstairs.*

BOLU. Smile, sister.

PEACE. I'm concentrating.

BOLU. You're doing great.

PEACE. No, I'm butchering it.

BOLU. What does that mean?

PEACE. I sound stupid. My pronunciation's all wrong and I feel like I'm ruining one of your memories.

BOLU. No it's perfect.

PEACE. I don't want to do it any more.

BOLU. Look at me. I believe in you. Do you remember the first time we made African porridge? What happened sister?

PEACE. I burnt it?

BOLU. You burnt it. And the second time. The one where I stood over your shoulder and gave you strict instructions to follow moment to moment? How did that one taste?

PEACE. Bad.

BOLU *and* PEACE *laugh.*

BOLU. It was very very bad, Peace.

PEACE. This isn't –

BOLU. So was the third attempt.

PEACE. – helping my confidence.

BOLU. But you didn't give up! And your fourth try was…?

PEACE. Pretty good.

BOLU. Eheh!

PEACE *laughs*.

I do not care if you are 'butchering' the pronunciation. I want to hear you try.

PEACE *rolls her eyes*.

PEACE. Okay.

BOLU. Okay.

They sing.

PEACE/BOLU. *Ọkin ọba ẹye*
An npe Ọ
Ọkin ọba ẹye
An npe
Ha, iwọ ẹyẹ mi
To ba ti sọ kalẹ, ṣe wa kọron ilẹ wa?
Haa Haa Haa
Ki inu rẹ dun
Haa Haa Ha

Ma jẹ ki awọn ọdẹ mu ọ
Ma jẹ ki awọn ọdẹ mu ọ

Haa Haa Haa
Ki inu rẹ dun
Haa Haa Haa
Ọkin Ọba Ẹyẹ

Ha, iwọ ẹyẹ mi
To ba na iyẹ apa rẹ nibo lo nlọ?
Ha, iwọ ẹyẹ mi
To ba ti sọ kalẹ, se wa kọrin ilẹ wa?

Ma je ki awọn ọdẹ mu ọ
Ma je ki awọn ọdẹ mu ọ

[*Black Crowned Crane*.
We are calling.
Black Crowned Crane.
We are calling.
Oh my bird. If you leave our land then where will you go?
Oh my bird. Will you bring food home or go and feed others?

Haa Haa Haa
Be happy.
Haa Haa Haa

Don't let the hunters catch you o.
Don't let the hunters catch you oh no no no no.
Haa Haa Haa
Be happy.
Haa Haa Haa
Black Crowned Crane.

Oh my bird. If you leave our land then where will you go.
Oh my bird. Will you bring food home or go and feed others.

Don't let the hunters catch you o.
Don't let the hunters catch you oh no no no no.]

During the song, FAVOUR *enters the room, but* PEACE *and* BOLU *are unaware.* FAVOUR *hangs back – watching.*

The song ends.

Note: Not all of the song needs to be sung here.

BOLU. See!

PEACE *is emotional.*

Sister?

PEACE. I'm fine, I'm… it's just, it's beautiful.

BOLU. My singing?

PEACE. No.

Beat. FAVOUR *watches* PEACE.

Can I hug you please?

BOLU. Of course.

PEACE *holds* BOLU *tight, like he's a life raft.*

PEACE. I'm so glad you're here.

The space rumbles and the song echoes, it is now more voices. The FATHER'S VOICE *is one of them.* FAVOUR *winces at the sound of it all. And nobody sees.*

FATHER'S VOICE. *Ole to ji kakaki ǫba, o ku i bi ti o fǫn.* Look at her…

BOLU (*to* PEACE). Look at you.

Scene Six

Thursday morning. FAVOUR, PEACE *and* ROY. PEACE *is dressed for work.*

PEACE. I think I love him. Bolu. Like 'I think I would dive in front of a car for him' kind of 'love him' already. That's that's really weird isn't? That's a bit fast.

ROY. Don't think so.

FAVOUR. It is.

FAVOUR *boils the kettle.*

ROY. Babe it's the whole point of spending time with him. It's a good thing. You should tell him.

PEACE. No, no… no. What if he doesn't say it back? What if he's like you?

ROY. I said it back.

PEACE. You paused.

ROY. No I / didn't –

PEACE. You paused babe.

ROY. Thirty seconds, twenty seconds even. You said it, I looked at you – with love in my eyes by the way – and thought 'oh this is big, this is nice, are we doing this, yes I'm doing this, here we go' – Bam – I love you too. Not even twenty seconds Peace. Ten seconds.

PEACE. It was a flipping awful time.

FAVOUR. Where is Bolu?

PEACE. Went for a walk about an hour ago, said he needed
to make calls. Okay I'm gonna head in. Mum – I've left
painkillers on the side table in case today's a bad day. And
I've ordered those blackout blinds. They should arrive this
afternoon.

PEACE *rushes to* FAVOUR, *holds her quickly and kisses her
on the cheek. Then rushes to* ROY *and kisses him.*

ROY. Have a good day.

PEACE *exits.* ROY *and* FAVOUR *are left alone.* ROY *opens
up his laptop to work.* FAVOUR *makes tea.*

FATHER'S VOICE. *Lé kì í jó kí oorun kun ojú.* 'A house does
not burn and fill the eyes with sleep.' We cannot ignore it.

FAVOUR *winces a little, then shakes off the pain.*

FAVOUR. How are you today, darling?

ROY *looks up and around the room.*

I'm talking to you Roy. There's nobody else here.

ROY. Yeah I know, I know… I'm fine thank you.

FAVOUR. Good, my dear.

FAVOUR *places a cup of tea in front of* ROY, *then goes back
to the kitchen.*

ROY *looks at the tea then back at* FAVOUR.

ROY (*teasing*). 'My dear' *and* a cup of tea…? No biscuits?

FAVOUR *rolls her eyes.*

Thank you.

FAVOUR *goes back to the kitchen.* ROY *shuts his laptop.*

How are you?

FAVOUR. Are you really asking?

ROY. No I just want my room back.

FAVOUR *laughs*. ROY *smiles, then –*

Seriously. How are you?

FAVOUR. Better than yesterday but not quite alright.

Pause.

It's loud. In my mind. And the worry doesn't help.

ROY. What is there to worry –

FAVOUR. I'm worried about Peace, Roy. And the strange boy that looks vaguely like her father. The stranger that Peace is so quick to love, despite the fact that he hasn't actually told us anything about himself. I am distressed because, besides me, nobody else seems to care.

ROY. You don't need to be. I have my eye on things.

FAVOUR. No you don't. You are always watching *me*. Always fighting me for Peace's attention.

ROY. Favour, I don't fight you for Peace's attention.

FAVOUR. It distracts you my dear, and it is very sad to watch but Peace doesn't mind so here we are.

ROY. If you actually want to talk about this –

FAVOUR. I don't care Roy, I'm used to you by now, I think of you as family.

ROY. Thank you. I also think –

FAVOUR. But that boy. The boy. There is something in him that is just not right, no? Has he said anything strange to you or Peace?

ROY. Like what?

FAVOUR. I don't know. He has been here a week, making memories – that I do not doubt she is paying for – burrowing his way into her life and gaining her trust and nobody is asking – why? What does he want?

ROY. Don't you think if Bolu was gonna do something bad he would have done it by now?

FAVOUR. Maybe. We can only hope so. She is grieving Roy,
we are still grieving, and that makes you vulnerable. You
know that. What else do we know about him besides his
name, occupation, and the city he lives in?

Pause.

ROY. Peace feels safe around him, she trusts him.

FAVOUR. We are the ones who keep her safe Roy. Try to
remember that. We are her family and we are on the same
side. He is the outsider.

Scene Seven

Thursday evening. An excited PEACE *talks as* FAVOUR
arranges the living area.

PEACE. Bolu's been teaching me loads of Yoruba sayings.

FAVOUR. Yes I've seen.

PEACE. He taught me *Ile ọba t'o jo, ẹwa lo busi* – which
means… erm 'When the king's palace burns down, the
palace he – no – the rebuilt palace is even more beautiful.'

FAVOUR. I know the saying.

PEACE. Well my pronunciation is –

FAVOUR. I understand you.

PEACE. It's clever right? He's clever.

FAVOUR. It just an old proverb. We all learnt them.

PEACE. He also taught me – *Ohun ti ájá ri to fi ngbó ko to eyi ti
aguntan-an fi nṣeran wo.*

FAVOUR. 'What a dog sees and barks at is nothing compared to
what the sheep ponders in silence.'

PEACE. Yes that's it, isn't that –

FAVOUR. It's a common saying Peace.

Pause.

PEACE *goes to speak but stops herself. She looks down at the ground. Her hand absentmindedly pats the dining table... stuttering and insistent.*

You know daughter, being here I've realised how much I was really struggling at the house, since you moved back in with Roy. I have been wondering –

PEACE. The sayings aren't common to me. They're foreign. That's why I'm trying to use them, because I want to *know* them. I am just – I just wanted to share – forget it.

Pause. FAVOUR *looks at* PEACE.

FAVOUR. I can speak Yoruba to you.

PEACE. Will you?

FAVOUR. I spoke it with your father.

PEACE. But you both never let me hear that. You didn't like it.

FAVOUR. You are remembering incorrectly. I didn't teach you because you were not interested in learning it.

PEACE. I heard him speak it to himself sometimes. He'd mutter words like that and then translate to himself do you remember?

FAVOUR. No darling.

PEACE. Do you not remember that? In the last –

FAVOUR. No Peace, can I talk to you about our living arrangements –

PEACE. *Ole to ji kakaki ọba, o ku i bi ti o fọn.*

FAVOUR. What?

PEACE. *Ole to ji kakaki ọba, o ku i bi ti o fọn.*

FAVOUR. Where did you hear that? From your father?

PEACE. No Bolu. It means –

FAVOUR. I know what the words mean, daughter. Please stop translating to me.

Pause.

PEACE. Sorry. Just…

FAVOUR. Are you okay?

PEACE. When you look at Bolu do you see dad? Dad but like, before… like… – I just really want to make him proud. Bolu. I just really want – I want to make him smile, because at the end it was so hard to… [*make Dad smile.*] Do you think he sees Bolu and me?

FATHER'S VOICE. You have to listen.

FAVOUR *looks at her daughter; there is a deep sadness.*

FAVOUR. I'm sorry. But no. I don't.

Scene Eight

Friday.

ROY *sits at the dining table working from his laptop.* BOLU *enters, phone to his ear, barely registering* ROY *as he speaks – as if he's at home.*

BOLU. *Tẹ jẹjẹ.* How bad is it? Are you able to take care of her? *Ko tiya.* Because I have things to do here. *Mama mi mọ nipa ẹ.* This will make things better for us. Just – *Jẹ kin ba wọn sọrọ.* Please, put her back on the phone. Why not? Okay, okay, the treatment – how much are they asking for? *What?*

FAVOUR *enters from the front door, carrying shopping.* BOLU *sees her. He speaks in a hushed voice.*

I have to go. *Ma pe e pada.* I'll get it to you shortly. Just…
sort it out for me, please.

BOLU *hangs up, stressed.* FAVOUR *smiles.*

FAVOUR. Your call sounded important. Did something happen
at home?

BOLU *is hesitant to share.*

BOLU. My mama had a small fall. She's had to go to hospital
again.

FAVOUR. Oh.

ROY. Oh.

FAVOUR *looks at* ROY – *pointedly.*

BOLU. It happens sometimes because of her old injuries. It
started back when I was a boy.

ROY. I'm sorry, man. You must be worried.

FAVOUR. Are you going to go home?

BOLU. Not yet no.

FAVOUR. I can't imagine Peace leaving me injured and alone
so she can go on the London Eye and ride red buses.

BOLU. She is not alone. She is at the hospital now with our
neighbours, they are good friends, and she understands.
Unfortunately I am exactly where I need to be.

ROY. Well, if there's any way we can help –

FAVOUR. I'm sure sweet Bolu does not expect you to give him
money Roy.

BOLU. Of course not. It is fine. Thank you both.

PEACE *enters, she looks flustered. She goes straight to the
kitchen and gets water.*

PEACE. Hello. Sorry. I'm back. Sorry.

BOLU. Welcome *Aburo arabinrin.*

PEACE. Everyone okay?

PEACE *downs the water.*

ROY. Bolu had some bad –

BOLU. We are all well. Thank you sister. How was your day?

PEACE. Yeah. Yeah, I just need a second, sorry.

ROY. Nine-E?

PEACE. She's just – she's exhausting that's all.

FAVOUR. What did she do?

PEACE. Gave a speech.

BOLU. Who? A / student?

FAVOUR. *During* your lesson?

PEACE. Yeah, yes, in the middle of my stupid PowerPoint. She stood on a table and launched into a speech.

ROY (*impressed*). *Oh shit.*

FAVOUR. And what did you do?

PEACE. I tried to send her out.

FAVOUR. Tried? Peace, how many times. She has to be expelled.

PEACE. Yes, Mum, but I've told you, she's not being troublesome in other classes, it's just mine. She won't be expelled unless I get her expelled. And I can't do that.

BOLU. Sorry, why is this student only troublesome in your class?

PEACE. Because I'm – because she thinks I'm – I don't know.

ROY. Well you do. It's because / you're –

PEACE. It's mainly because she doesn't like what I teach.

FAVOUR. She doesn't like history.

ROY. It's because Peace is Black and –

FAVOUR. She doesn't let Peace get through a lesson. She shouts, writes messages on the table, plays music out loud. She is a lost cause but Peace rarely reports her, so she thinks her behavior is acceptable.

(*To* PEACE.) If you let her undermine you, you will continue to look weak in front of your students.

BOLU. What did the student say? In this speech?

PEACE. It was a lesson on World War II and she stood up and listed the years that countries gained independence from the British Empire. She shouted '*India 1947!, Ghana 1957!, Nigeria, Jamaica, Kenya; if they were still part of the empire where are their faces? They fought but there is no mention of them.*' And then she just kept shouting 'Where are their faces?'

FAVOUR. What kind of child?

BOLU. She sounds –

PEACE. Troubled. Yeah –

BOLU. No. Clever.

ROY. Oh she's very clever.

PEACE *looks at* ROY.

BOLU. And the student is Black?

PEACE. Yeah. Yeah she's Black.

ROY. There's only two of them in that school, so it's a lot of pressure.

PEACE. I don't feel any pressure. And there are five of us, that are not [*white*] – there's five.

BOLU (*puzzled*). But this student is right. Is she not?

PEACE. No. I mean sure yeah – but not really, not completely. What she's asking for isn't required. It's not in the lesson plans so – the thing is she – she –

BOLU. Can you not change the lesson?

PEACE. Why is it up to me to change the lessons?

FAVOUR. It's not.

PEACE. I understand she wants to know these things, but it's not going to be in the exam. I can't change the tests. It's not my job to teach them what they want to know, it's my job to teach them what they *need* to know. So they pass. She has to pass. She has to.

And I can't help her when she is constantly talking about things we're not meant to be studying.

BOLU. But it is a good question, is it not? About the faces.

PEACE. Yeah sure. It's a good question. But –

FAVOUR. The question is irrelevant.

BOLU. How is truth irrelevant?

PEACE. It's just – complicated. You wouldn't understand but there are – there are certain requirements over here and I can't deviate from them, I can't. Especially for the one troublesome Black student – I can't do that – I can't just –

BOLU. Roy, what do you think?

ROY. Oh I don't want to –

FAVOUR. Roy is not there.

ROY. Actually no, I think er – obviously the situation is nuanced. Peace is the *only* Black teacher and that girl is the only Black student. So I get that she's looking at her like some sort of symbol or whatever. And sure maybe she feels a bit disillusioned by –

PEACE. *Disillusioned?*

ROY. There's probably a better w–

PEACE. You've never said that word.

ROY. Right, because you've been sensitive about –

PEACE. I'm not –

ROY. Babe. I'm just saying we all know what it was like to be one the 'onlys' and sometimes that means you attack the wrong people.

FAVOUR. What kind of parent lets their child misbehave like that?

PEACE. Thank you.

FAVOUR. Is this girl Caribbean? She must be Caribbean. Most probably one of your people Roy. A *Ji-mai-kan*.

ROY. Favour, you know I'm / not Jamaican.

PEACE. He's / not –

FAVOUR. It was a joke. Mr Marley.

BOLU. She is just a young girl asking you a question –

PEACE. You put your hand up to ask a question, you stand on a table to make a statement. And don't be fooled by her age – she is a fourteen-year-old that recites political facts like it's the alphabet. She doesn't look young, she looks tired – because she spends all day fighting and rallying and trying to force me to do the same and I feel sorry for her, I *do* but like… Has everyone eaten? Shall we go out for dinner?

ROY. Bolu is the African educational system completely transparent?

PEACE. Bolu can't speak for all of Africa.

ROY. Don't do that Peace.

BOLU. No, it's not.

FAVOUR. We all know how the world works. That girl is doing this because she knows that you will not deal with her as any other teacher would do.

BOLU. Okay, but –

FAVOUR. Let her try this nonsense with 'Mr Timothy Smith'. Let her try this nonsense with 'Samantha' and 'Felicity-May'. There is a curriculum. If she wants to know more then she should tell her parents to teach her more at home.

BOLU. Did you teach Peace the truth at home?

FAVOUR. Excuse me?

BOLU. Di– di– di– Sorry one moment.

   BOLU *looks down at the ground*.

ROY. Don't we all just pretend the books are right and then teach ourselves outside of school when we get to our twenties anyway?

FAVOUR (*to* PEACE). You need to be more strict.

PEACE. I will.

FAVOUR. You need to set better boundaries.

PEACE. I will. I'll try Mummy.

BOLU (*to himself*). No, you need to –

PEACE. What…? What?

   BOLU *looks at* PEACE.

BOLU. She didn't ask you to change the tests. She asked you to add more faces to the picture. Perhaps, sister, you need to do what she asked.

   The beating of a single drum. It rings out, then another; it grows until its rhythmic and fast flowing into –

Scene Nine

Saturday.

Proverbs we have already heard from the FATHER'S VOICE *overlap each other chaotically.*

PEACE *and* FAVOUR *are in the living area.* PEACE *is at the table surrounded by papers and books on British Black history. She types into her laptop.* FAVOUR *speaks –*

FAVOUR. Yes or no Peace?

The noise quiets.

PEACE. Erm Well – erm…

FAVOUR. Yes or no Peace?

PEACE. I don't know Mum. It's not really a choice I can make on my own.

FAVOUR. It makes so much more sense than what we're doing already? Does it not?

PEACE. Yeah.

FAVOUR. What do you mean 'yeah'?

PEACE. I mean yes Mummy, I guess it's –

FAVOUR. And the houses are so close anyway. I would just be closer.

PEACE *gets up to open a window.*

Are you listening to me?

PEACE. I am… I'm just concerned that Roy –

FAVOUR. Roy would be fine. After all, he's been eating all the food I prepare, he's been enjoying how I've kept the house orderly and clean. Are we not getting along very well? I've stopped complaining when he puts on the terrible films where the cartoons fight. Though he really is too old to be watching cartoons, daughter. It's distressing.

PEACE. It's anime, Mum.

FAVOUR. That is just a sophisticated way of saying cartoons. My point is – it is working.

PEACE. It's working now yes, but moving in permanently Mum. That's –

FAVOUR. Not *permanently*. Not forever. God forbid. Just a while. Do you not want me with you? You have not minded, have you daughter?

PEACE. No. The thing is Mum, Roy wants to… He's actually thinking about – he's asked…

Pause.

FAVOUR. What…? *What?* You are scaring me.

PEACE. Nothing serious. I just know now's not the right time to talk to him about it. Because of work. Because he's got a lot on. I can tell him that you asked. Soon. Just not now.

FAVOUR *assesses* PEACE.

FAVOUR. Okay then daughter. Tell him in a few days. And remind him it is not a crime to want to be with your child. I wish my mother had wanted to spend as much time with me.

PEACE *looks at* FAVOUR.

PEACE.…You never talk about your mother.

And FAVOUR *doesn't want to now either.*

FAVOUR. These lights. They are terrible. Much too bright. If I do move in, they have to go.

They will be back late this evening?

PEACE. Yes.

FAVOUR. Good. I have you to myself.

Scene Ten

Saturday.

Sweet sweet Afrobeats. ROY *and* BOLU *enter the house. They have both been drinking, but* ROY *is more drunk than* BOLU. *They sing the lyrics to the Nigerian song 'Jantamanta' by Mavins.* ROY *gets louder.*

BOLU. Shhhh. We will wake everybody up.

ROY. Let them wake up! It's my house.

BOLU. You don't mean that –

ROY. No I don't. If anyone comes down, can you pretend that was you?

BOLU *laughs*.

BOLU. Well tonight was entertaining. Thank you Roy.

ROY. We're not done yet. You're not even that drunk.

BOLU. You are drunk enough for the both of us.

ROY. Come on! It's been great having some guy time.

BOLU. Guy time?

ROY. Yes that's what it is – Guy time! We're having guy time!

BOLU. Okay. Okay. What are we drinking?

ROY. My man! Beers in the fridge.

BOLU *goes to the fridge as* ROY *stumbles over to the dining table, which is covered in books and notes.* BOLU *returns with two beers; he places one before* ROY.

Look. Peace's new lesson plans. She hears you.

BOLU *and* ROY *read bits.* BOLU *nods.* ROY *studies* BOLU *as* BOLU *picks up a book.*

You know what I think? I think I think you're great. I think *that's* what I think. I think I think you're my favourite one of Peace's relatives.

BOLU. Okay... Thank you.

ROY. It used to be her dad but he's dead now. God rest his soul. I shouldn't say that. Apologies.

BOLU. You are fine.

ROY. Not that we had any particular relationship. He was quiet. Honestly he seemed a bit depressed. And lonely. But he seemed to like the fact that I was around. He didn't make me feel unwelcome or anything. You knew where you stood with him.

BOLU. You and Favour, you don't really talk.

ROY. Not any more, no.

BOLU. Why?

> ROY *shrugs*.

ROY. First time I met Favour, I was so eager. I brought round flowers. Then I said 'hello Aunty' and I did the prostate thing.

BOLU. Prostate?

ROY. You know the prostate thing?

BOLU. *What?*

ROY. The thing!

> ROY *lies across the floor*

BOLU (*laughing*). Oh prostrate!

ROY. Yeah.

BOLU. And what did Favour do?

ROY. She looked down at me and said 'My name is Favour not Aunty and please don't lie across my carpet.'

> BOLU *laughs*. ROY *laughs too*.

> Still, it weren't too bad. Things got worse as your dad got worse.

BOLU. Do you know many of Peace's relatives?

ROY. Nope.

> BOLU *thinks*.

> Right Bolu, you have to tell me her name.

BOLU. Not this again.

ROY. Nah, you get this look in your eye. Like there's someone you need to get back to. I know that look. I'm the king of that look.

BOLU. The only person I need to get back to is my mother.

ROY. Right.

BOLU. I spoke to her again today – she's better. She should not have fallen, but she gets distracted, she worries.

ROY. Because you're over here?

BOLU. What about your family? You don't mention them much.

ROY. Two sets of aunties and uncles. Grandparents in Trinidad. They're the best. Other grandparents live in Barbados now, they're alright. Mum died when I was young, Dad died when I was not so young. Eight.

BOLU. I am sorry.

ROY. Don't be. People die. We know this. Don't really go though do they. I can hear Dad when I want. And I'm sure I'd hear Mum if I knew what her voice was like. I'm sure she speaks. My main family though, that's Peace. She's my person. For better or worse.

BOLU. Tell me, why aren't you two married?

ROY. You don't need to be married to love someone.

BOLU. No, but still. Have you ever asked? Or do you think she would say no?

ROY *thinks*.

Something to do with your break-up, last year?

ROY. She told you about that? I don't know. If we did get married I'm not even sure what I'd be marrying into. I'm an equations guy and I'm not even close to figuring out how to fit into all… that.

Pause.

Has she told you about why she's afraid to fly?

BOLU. Yes, claustraphobic and afraid of heights, right?

ROY. Ah, but she hasn't told you about the game? The games they played when she was a kid and how every time –

Pause.

I see what you did there. You got me to stop talking about
you, again. You're good at that. Fishing and hiding.

BOLU. I'm just listening to you Roy. *Akì í dáké ̣ká ̣sìwí; a kì í
wò sùn-ùn ká dáràn.*

A person cannot misspeak, if they are quiet and –

ROY. Oh yeah Peace said you do that, start speaking in 'Ye olde
Yoruba proverbs' out of nowhere. She deflects too you know,
but you're better at it. You're a lot cleverer than I thought
you'd be.

BOLU *laughs*.

BOLU. Oh you thought I would be dumb?

ROY. No – See, *see* – that's what I mean. I knew you'd shake
things up round here, in fact I hoped you would. I just didn't
know it would be intentional.

BOLU. You should drink some water.

ROY *is suddenly serious*.

ROY. You didn't come here for any money did you?

BOLU*'s face drops. Pause*.

BOLU. That's what you thought?

ROY. No, maybe, at first but... I *have* been watching you Bolu.
And see, what I don't get about you is...

BOLU. Yes Roy?

ROY. What I don't get about you is you never ask us about your
dad. You don't like us talking about him. You never carry on
the conversations about him, never ask what he was like. You
never ask any questions about *him*.

BOLU. Because he made his decision a long time ago – that is
all I need to know.

ROY. And *that's* why you don't make sense Bolu. Peace made
a Facebook post about her dad a year after he died and
someone showed it to you, that's how you found her, right?

BOLU. Yes, that is right.

ROY. None of them were really on socials, so when that picture popped up – I mean you were looking for him, weren't you? You were looking for your dad, and you must have been looking for him your whole life, yes?

BOLU. Yes.

ROY suddenly seems sober and piercing.

ROY. Why were you searching for someone you wanted nothing to do with?

Beat.

BOLU. It's complicated.

ROY. Right. And not for me to know is it? But I've got a feeling. You won't hurt Peace will you?

Pause.

BOLU. Never intentionally.

ROY. That's good. Because I love her. Against my better judgement.

ROY smiles, so drunk.

Because she won't choose me in the end. Nah. Never gonna choose Roy.

Slight pause.

Might choose you though.

ROY looks at BOLU.

Because of *that* face.

BOLU. You are very drunk Roy.

Pause.

Are you two not happy?

ROY. Sometimes. The rest of the time I think we're just… in love.

BOLU. I see. And that is enough?

Pause.

ROY. *Very very clever.* I… I did ask her to marry me once and… hold on a second, I think I'm gonna be sick.

ROY *runs offstage and* BOLU *chuckles, watching after him. And then the drums.* BOLU *stands and begins looking through the living-room drawers once again. Finally he finds things. Seemingly unimportant. He hides them on his person and heads upstairs.*

ROY *comes back into the living room. He stumbles onto the sofa and falls asleep. Moments later* PEACE *enters in her pyjamas. She looks at* ROY, *before lying down next to him. Without waking up,* ROY *holds her and they rest. The stage darkens. Quiet.*

Scene Eleven

Sunday.

FAVOUR *enters. Determinedly, she turns on the kitchen radio. Music is interrupted by white noise and the muffled* FATHER'S VOICE, *but* FAVOUR *adjust the settings until it's just a song. She looks toward the living room door leading to upstairs and turns the music even louder. She starts to clean. And sing. Maybe even dance. Think – OutKast 'Hey Ya!' Finally* BOLU *enters.* FAVOUR *turns the music off.*

FAVOUR. Oh! Sorry, did I wake you? I forgot you were here.

BOLU. It is fine. I am usually up by this time anyway Ma. Where is Peace?

FAVOUR. Out. She left with Roy about twenty minutes ago. Why?

BOLU. I wanted to speak with her but never mind.

Pause.

I will go back to the room.

FAVOUR. I hope it was worth it?

BOLU. Pardon?

FAVOUR. Roy looked as bad as you do, after your night yesterday.

BOLU. Oh yes.

FAVOUR. You're having fun eh?

BOLU. Yes, Ma.

FAVOUR. Your trip has been all you dreamed it would be?

BOLU. Yes, Ma.

FAVOUR. Good. As long as you have got what you came for.

> BOLU *turns to go, then stops. Beat. He faces* FAVOUR *again.*

BOLU. What do you mean by that, Ma?

FAVOUR. What?

BOLU. What do you mean by 'what I came for'?

FAVOUR. Nothing in particular.

BOLU. Of course. How is your head Ma? Your migraines?

FAVOUR. The pain comes in waves.

BOLU. And does loud music help?

FAVOUR. Believe it or not, sometimes yes. I wanted to tell you. I read some of your articles this morning. I found them online.

BOLU. You did? What did you think?

FAVOUR. They were not for me.

BOLU. Ah. A shame.

FAVOUR. Too wordy. There was one – what was it…? 'The execution of identity and the pain of our performance.'

BOLU. Yes. That one is one of my favorites.

FAVOUR. Not great. Very perplexing. An unnecessary attempt at being clever. I could not work out what you wanted your reader to learn. I wished you would be direct.

BOLU. Well. I try to write things that make readers look at themselves, not me. If they are not ready to do that, what I write will seem like nonsense.

FAVOUR. Yes. But that doesn't seem wise to me. I am of the opinion that if you have something important to say, you say it plainly. That way everyone knows where they stand.

Beat. BOLU *makes a decision.*

BOLU. Why were you researching me?

FAVOUR. Hm?

BOLU. Why were you researching me Ma, online?

FAVOUR. I wanted to know more about you.

BOLU. But *why*? Because you don't trust me. Ma.

FAVOUR. No. No I don't. Sweet Bolu.

Pause.

BOLU. Shall we just have a real conversation? I am ready to stop pretending if you are?

FAVOUR. I am not the one pretending.

BOLU. You have asked me to talk plainly, but will not drop your own act?

FAVOUR. You look at me strangely. I don't like it.

BOLU. I have found you very impressive. Your relationship with Peace. How you have kept yourself here. The way you manipulate situations. I now wonder if you manipulated my father.

FAVOUR. Oh you think I manipulated your father into marrying me? Is that what you're saying? Is that what you want? To blame me because he abandoned you and your mother?

Pause.

What your father did. That was before Peace and I, you know
that. I'm ashamed to say he never mentioned you. Your father
never gave you a second thought.

Beat. The faint echo of the drums.

BOLU. I was so young.

Pause.

Would you like to know how I got into journalism Ma? That
man, my father, he left no trace of where he was going. No
word with relatives or friends. For years I would type his
name into computers looking for some clue of where he
was and there was nothing. No profile, no pictures. Nothing.
Everyone has asked me not to be angry but it is deeper than
that. Stronger than that. You know all this time I had never
been certain, but as soon as I saw you, I knew. How bold
you are to distrust me when I have stayed here keeping *your*
secrets.

FAVOUR. I have no secrets.

BOLU. I was a small boy. Young enough that you hoped
I would not remember.

FAVOUR. I tire of this conversation / let's leave it –

BOLU. But I have been putting the pieces together. The first
time he left for England, Mama she did not cry much.
I imagine because he told her he would come back to us or
bring us to him. I imagine she was proud. But the day he
came back... I was wearing my best clothes the day he came
back. I was not allowed to play outside because Mama did
not want me to mess them up. She was excited. I wanted
her to lift me but she couldn't because her hands were full.
Then – when Father came home I remember Mama crying.
So I knew, he was not staying. I remember looking at Mama
crying and wishing he had never come back. But he had to...
didn't he? And I couldn't speak. I stopped speaking that day.
Tell me, was it hard to watch?

FAVOUR. I don't know what you –

BOLU. Is it still hard to look at me? You didn't look at me then.

Beat.

FAVOUR. Why are you here Bolu?

BOLU. You are afraid? You should be. I remember you.

ACT TWO

Scene One

The living area is now full of boxes.

And the song 'Black Crowned Crane' begins.

Ọkin ọba ẹye
An npe Ọ
Ọkin ọba ẹye
An npe Ha…

The song goes on but this time the melody is full, many voices ringing out and the bass reverberating. Stamps are added. This simple song now sounds otherworldy and timeless. The FATHER *speaks –*

FATHER'S VOICE. Only one day brings disgrace to a person; the shame is felt every day.

PEACE *enters. She does not hear the music.*

PEACE. Mummy?

Pause

Mummy?!

FATHER'S VOICE. Shhhhh.

The music fades.

PEACE. Mummy!

FAVOUR (*from off*). Yes.

FAVOUR *enters.*

PEACE *is remembering/recalling this moment, but* FAVOUR *is there – reliving it.*

Peace, I've told you to stop playing with the moving boxes.

PEACE. Help me make a castle please Mummy.

FAVOUR. Look at this mess.

PEACE. Can you help me?

FAVOUR. You have so many toys and yet you play with boxes. Why do you want to make a castle?

PEACE. For Bobo to live in.

FAVOUR. Your Bobo doesn't need anywhere to live. He is not real.

PEACE. Yes he is.

FAVOUR. No he's not.

Pause.

Why can't your friend just live in a normal house?

PEACE. I wanted him to stay here with us but he's too homesick, so I'm bringing his home here.

FAVOUR. Are you now?

PEACE. Daddy said that Bobo's home is full of riches.

FAVOUR. Your father indulges you.

PEACE. Daddy said that the whole country is made of money but they don't always use it the best. So I'm gonna use the money to make a castle.

FAVOUR. Where is your friend from?

PEACE. Nigeria, like us. Except he's allowed to go back home. He's only here because we're not.

FAVOUR. Who told you we are not allowed to go back home?

PEACE. Daddy said we're never going there because you'll get upset.

FAVOUR. Your father said that?

FATHER'S VOICE. I said that.

PEACE. He did.

FATHER'S VOICE. I should have said more.

PEACE. He said it *very* quietly.

FAVOUR. I won't get upset.

PEACE. You don't like talking about Nigeria, Mum.

FAVOUR. No.

PEACE. Why? What's it like? Mummy? What's it like?

FAVOUR. Where I was, it was dark.

PEACE. Well I'm not afraid of the dark.

FAVOUR. It's packed.

PEACE. What does that mean?

FAVOUR. It is packed with people, it is unpleasant and crowded.

PEACE. It can't be like that everywhere.

FAVOUR. Everywhere your mother remembers, daughter. It is full of people and struggle, full of questions and pain. The pain makes them unkind. Mummy doesn't want to go back there.

PEACE. *I* want to go.

FAVOUR. No you don't.

PEACE. Yes I do.

FAVOUR. It is hard to get there daughter.

PEACE. I don't mind.

FAVOUR. You have to get on a plane for hours and hours.

PEACE. Planes are fun Mummy, at the end of being on the plane I get to be anywhere in the world.

FAVOUR. Planes are dark and cold and go high. Some people never make it to where they want to go.

PEACE. You're afraid Mummy.

That's okay. You don't have to go. You can stay here with
Daddy and I can take Bobo home.

FAVOUR. I thought you were building Bobo a castle here?

PEACE. Yeah but he can't live in it forever. Because it's just
boxes Mummy.

FAVOUR. You are so clever my darling.

If you're going to fly you need to be ready.

FAVOUR *and* PEACE *look at each other. Beat. Then*
FAVOUR *is back reliving the memory.*

Would you like to play a game?

PEACE. Yeah.

FAVOUR. Yes Mummy.

PEACE. Yes Mummy.

FAVOUR. Okay. Mummy is going to show you the flying game.
Okay?

PEACE. Okay Mummy.

PEACE *continues watching* FAVOUR.

FAVOUR. First of all, we will make this box the plane.

PEACE. The whole plane?

FAVOUR. Yes the *whole plane*. You are the traveller, so you
have to get in it.

Pause.

Get in.

Pause.

Play with Mummy darling. Welcome aboard. This is your
flight to Nigeria. This journey will take seven hours. Please
take your seat.

PEACE. Like this?

FAVOUR. Yes sweetheart. Now listen to Mummy. I'm going to... lock the plane. Okay?

PEACE. Okay.

FAVOUR. And this is a night-time flight so we have to turn off the lights.

The room darkens.

PEACE....Mummy – ?

FAVOUR. You have to stay in your seat, you have to stay because we are taking off now.

PEACE. Mum –

FAVOUR. Do you feel that? The plane goes very high and it shakes. And then it goes still. And you cannot get out.

PEACE. I think I get it now.

Pause.

Mummy I get it now.

FAVOUR. It's a long flight my darling, so you have to wait till it's done.

PEACE. Okay. Okay.

Beat. FAVOUR *turns to go.*

Are you going Mummy?

FAVOUR. You said you could go without me, daughter. So it's just you now, and your friend.

PEACE. Can you let me out?

FAVOUR. No daughter. Not yet.

FATHER'S VOICE. Ohhhh my child. Ọjọ́ kan là ḿbàjẹ́, ọjọ́ gbogbo lara ńtini. Can you hear me?

FAVOUR. Not yet.

FAVOUR *exits.*

FATHER'S VOICE. Can you hear me?

> PEACE *can hear knocking. Small at first, then bigger. It intertwines with drums, building and becoming irregular. A box placed on a high surface starts to teeter... We hear the* FATHER, *and his raspy last words –*

> Sorry, I'm sorry, I'm so – sorry I'm, I'm, I'm – I'm –

> *And just as the box starts to fall,* PEACE *lunges for it.*

Scene Two

Tuesday.

Drums. The boxes are replaced by BOLU*'s packed belongings.*

FAVOUR *is waiting in the living room.*

FATHER'S VOICE. I am the Father of Secrets, you are the Mother of Mystery.

> BOLU *enters.*

> I am the Father of Lies. You are the Mother of Deceit. *Iyawo?! Iyawo?!*

FAVOUR. Hello sweet Bolu.

BOLU. Why are my things down here?

FAVOUR. I packed them. It was too messy upstairs.

BOLU. You touched my belongings?

FAVOUR. You are welcome.

BOLU. Did you go into my suitcase?

FAVOUR. Why? Are you hiding something?

> *Beat.*

BOLU. I told you that you had one day.

FAVOUR. *You* do not give me ultimatums.

BOLU. You had one day to speak to Peace and your day is up.

FAVOUR. Clearly you and I have struggled to understand each other's intentions. You have made me some kind of villain in your head. My motivation has always been, and will always be, my love for my daughter. There is nothing I would not do to keep her safe.

BOLU. I am done talking with you.

FAVOUR. Bolu please. Whatever kind of person you think I am, whatever you think I have done, you are wrong. You are wrong about me. If you leave my daughter alone I can help you.

BOLU. Help me?

FAVOUR. I have an offer to make you.

BOLU. The answer is no. I will be waiting upstairs.

FAVOUR. *Ọmọ ale*.

    BOLU *smiles*.

BOLU. You know very well that I am not a bastard.

FAVOUR. But you are a thief.

    Pause.

    I did look. At your *things*. I know what you have been doing.

    BOLU *shakes his head and goes to leave*.

    Your mother, how is she?

BOLU. You dare speak about my mother?

FAVOUR. After her fall? I heard you say the hospital bills were expensive. I imagine it is a struggle for you to look after her and yourself. Financially.

BOLU. *Ajẹ ni o*.

FAVOUR. You must want to make it easier for her, yes?

BOLU. You hear me? You are a witch.

FAVOUR. Bolu who is the most important person to you?
Truly? I can make it so your mother's life is easy. I can give
you money – now – your father's life insurance. And I will
continue to send more. Just so long as you stay away.

BOLU *shakes his head again, disbelieving.*

You haven't seen how much yet.

FAVOUR *holds out an envelope.* BOLU *looks at her.*

Take it. Just have a look.

Pause.

BOLU *takes it. He looks inside…*

I never allowed myself to think about what it was like for
you. Growing up without your father. The truth is you
deserve the money. All of it is yours by right. And my
husband… He would have wanted you to have it. I did lie to
you. I said your father never gave you a second thought, but
he did.

Whisperings of the FATHER.

He cried for you. When he thought I couldn't see. He missed
you.

BOLU. He… he didn't know me.

FAVOUR. You were his firstborn, Bolu. He loved you. And he
wanted to make things right.

Pause.

If he could see, who you grew into, he would be so proud of
you. Because you are good. I can see that. Peace can see that.
Whatever part of you that doesn't hate him should honour
what he would have asked of you. Let life be easy. Take the
money and go.

BOLU *looks at the envelope, then at* FAVOUR.

PEACE *enters.*

PEACE. Hey I –

> BOLU *drops the envelope on the ground. He takes a step back. Beat.* PEACE *senses something is wrong.*

> (*To* FAVOUR.) I left work early to pick up the bits you asked for… Mum are you feeling any better?

> FAVOUR *and* BOLU *look at one another. Pause.* PEACE *goes to pick up the envelope.*

BOLU. Sister. I need to talk to you.

FAVOUR. Peace. Help.

> *Drums.* FAVOUR *winces.*

PEACE. What is it?

FAVOUR. Help.

BOLU. Can we go somewhere –

PEACE. Wait Bolu. Mum? Is something wrong?

> FAVOUR *looks at* PEACE *with fear in her eyes.*

FAVOUR. My head hurts.

BOLU. Can we talk?

> FAVOUR *is trembling. And the drums continue.*

PEACE. Mum look at me? What's happening? Is it –

FAVOUR. My head hurts Peace.

PEACE. Okay. Just look –

> FAVOUR *puts her hands to her temples. She cries out –*

FAVOUR. MY HEAD. IT HURTS.

> PEACE *runs over to her mum, who is now crouched on the floor, her head in her hands.*

PEACE. Okay, it's okay, Mummy. Okay –

BOLU. Peace please can –

PEACE. Bolu wait! Mum look – I'm here. I'm here, / don't worry.

BOLU. She is fine.

PEACE. / I'm right here.

FAVOUR. Turn off the lights.

PEACE. I'm doing it. I'm turning them off. Look I'm doing it.

> PEACE *runs about the stage, dimming the lights.* BOLU *stands there watching. The drums are heavy and chaotic.*

> Bolu help me get the other –

BOLU. But she is fine –

PEACE. Help me! / Help me with –

FAVOUR. It's too much – It's too much – It's too much – too much!

PEACE. She's in pain, we have to – we have to fix it!

FAVOUR. *It hurts it hurts it hurts it hurts it –*

PEACE. It's okay. I'm here. We're okay. We're okay. With me. With me now, with me. With me.

> PEACE *leans her head against* FAVOUR*'s. She puts her hands over her mother's hands and the two rock together back and forth. The room is dark and* BOLU *stands watching them.*

> It's okay. it's okay.

> *The drums quieten. Eventually* PEACE *and* FAVOUR *still, their eyes locked.*

FATHER'S VOICE. She has to listen –

> FAVOUR *whimpers.*

FAVOUR. I can't –

PEACE. Shhhh. Stay with me.

> *The drums stop. Silence.*

FAVOUR. Daughter. I need to tell you something.

Scene Three

Not long after. PEACE *and* BOLU *stand far apart.*

PEACE. She's upstairs.

BOLU. Does she do that a lot?

PEACE. We don't need to talk about it.

BOLU. It's not normal sister.

PEACE. Don't.

Beat.

She just… She told me about you.

BOLU. She told you the truth?

PEACE. Yes.

BOLU. What did she say?

Pause. BOLU *and* PEACE *watch each other.*

What did she –

PEACE. She told me that she knew about you the whole time.
She was there, in Nigeria when my dad left you and your
mum. She told me you've tried to get in touch before, but
they decided to hide you from me long ago.

BOLU *nods, waiting.*

BOLU. Is that it?

PEACE. She told me that you blame her for my father leaving.

BOLU. Nothing else?

PEACE. That you are angry at her.

BOLU. Of course I am angry at her, the woman is evil.

Pause.

PEACE. Did you attack her Bolu?

BOLU. What?

PEACE. Before she had her migraine, did you attack her?

BOLU. No. No I spoke to her.

PEACE. She says you said she manipulated my dad, she says you grabbed her.

BOLU. No. Well, yes I said *that* but I didn't touch her. You know I would never do that.

PEACE. Do I?

BOLU. Of course you do.

PEACE. Did you... did you threaten her for money?

BOLU. Peace. No.

PEACE. There was money in the envelope though. Wasn't there Bolu?

BOLU. Yes. Yes of course there was but th– th– that was her.

PEACE. And you had it, when I walked in *you* were holding it.

BOLU. No. No yes b– but she... she is twisting things. She is –

PEACE. She's afraid of you. She's scared of you.

BOLU. This is laughable.

PEACE. You have to leave.

BOLU. Peace, come on.

PEACE. I've been too trusting with you and ultimately you're a stranger.

BOLU. I – I am your bro–

PEACE. We went through your suitcase.

Pause.

I found my mum's bracelet.

PEACE *holds the item up to show* BOLU.

I found my mum's bracelet, which you *stole*, and – You took old pictures, and letters addressed to Dad, letters addressed to me, you'd taken my things.

BOLU. O– O– okay. That l– looks bad, I– I can understand that but just trust me that –

PEACE. *Trust you*? Trust you when you're stealing from me?

BOLU. Y– y– you're not l– l– listening.

PEACE. I've been so stupid. She said – she said there'd be something though. She said you / were dangerous.

BOLU. Let – let me – let me tell you / why I –

PEACE. And she was right. What were you planning? Some big scam? Steal our identities? Take all our money – what was it?

BOLU. I – I didn't come here / to be insulted –

PEACE. It was never about *me* was it? / You just needed me.

BOLU. I w– w– w will / not be –

PEACE. You know what just take it.

BOLU. I don't –

PEACE. Have the money, brother.

BOLU. I– I– I–

    BOLU *can't get his words out.*

PEACE. Take whatever you came for and go back home, just leave me –

BOLU. WILL YOU LET ME SPEAK!

    Beat. BOLU *breathes.*

    That is… Of course – Of course that is your conclusion. That we big, bad, native Africans, we only care about money, because we are so corrupt.

    BOLU *laughs to himself.*

    So that's how she wants to get away with it? The age-old narrative. I came here to steal from you because you are so rich. In your wonderful home-away-from-home and I am so very poor in my poor nation with my poor people. Your nation. Your people. You think I came to *take* from you?

PEACE. What do mean 'get away with it'?

BOLU. You think I want *your* life?

PEACE. That's not what I said.

BOLU. You did. You do. Because the unspoken rule is that you are a better African if you manage to get out of Africa. Why wouldn't I want your life? Is that not what our dear father believed? And for this life he gave his soul to the devil. It is so... shall I tell you what I see when I look at your life? You are rootless.

PEACE. Excuse me?

BOLU. Rootless. Your mother tongue is confused in your mouth, your heritage is hidden and your bedtime stories are anecdotes to make sure that you behave. You don't even recognise your heroes. Years, Peace. Years and years I searched... and you are so disappointing sister. Would you like me to tell you why I took those things? Would you like me to explain why I took the bracelet?

Pause.

FAVOUR (*from off*). Peace?

PEACE. Yes Mummy.

FAVOUR (*from off*). Is everything okay?

PEACE. I'm fine.

PEACE *looks at* BOLU.

Get out of this house.

Rumbling drums.

Scene Four

A few days later. Friday. Any evidence of BOLU*'s stay is gone.*
FAVOUR *has successfully reorganised and reordered the whole
house.*

PEACE. Her migraines are worse. She's up through the night,
she's crying all the time.

ROY. Is she?

PEACE. I hear her.

ROY. Right.

PEACE. I don't know what to do to make her better.

Pause.

Are you still angry at me?

ROY. You kicked him out without letting him explain Peace.

PEACE. I shouldn't have let him come in the first place.

ROY. But you wanted to meet him, there was a reason –

PEACE. I was confused, I was grieving. It was too soon to
shake things up after Dad dying. It's not like Mum didn't try
with Bolu, she tried really hard.

ROY. So you're just never gonna speak to him again?

PEACE. I don't want to, Roy.

ROY. Okay.

PEACE. Have *you*? Spoken to him?

ROY. No, no course not.

Slight pause.

I've checked in on him.

PEACE. Are you serious? After what he said Roy? After what
he did? He stole from us. He threatened Mum.

ROY. I just want you to think about the situation for a minute. It doesn't make sense Peace. None of it makes sense. He didn't take any money from you. He took pictures, keepsakes. What would he do with your mum's old bracelet?

PEACE. I don't know. I don't need to know –

ROY. Don't you think you should hear him out?

PEACE. You said it might be a scam. When he first messaged, you said careful these people will scam you.

ROY. I did not say –

PEACE. You did. You said people over there are always looking for Western relatives, you said don't trust these random men from –

ROY. I didn't say it *like* that – I was trying to make you laugh, I was – okay, maybe I did but – I changed my mind and, and I've spent time with him. So have you, you know him better than that.

PEACE. My mum is traumatised.

ROY. By what?! It can't be as straightforward as she's telling you. Peace you don't have to accept everything she says at face value. Ask her *some* questions. She hasn't explained lying about Bolu, even after you said he got in contact. She's hiding –

PEACE. What has he said to you?

ROY. It's not about what he's said Peace, it's about you – Listen I don't wanna be the… When he tracked you down. When I said that he might try to sca– I'm such an idiot – shit – anyway – When he sent you that message and told you who he was, and you saw that picture of him and his mum – You couldn't stop crying Peace. You were looking at his face and… you couldn't stop crying.

PEACE. So?

ROY. You need to make it make sense.

PEACE. I want to change the subject.

ROY. Of course you do.

PEACE. I want to change the subject. We can talk about anything else.

ROY. Yeah sure let's do this again. Shall we talk about my job offer Peace? I had to give my boss an answer yesterday, remember?

PEACE. Shit... I forgot.

ROY. No you didn't. But that's fine.

PEACE. Ask them for a few more days and I'll –

ROY. I can't do that.

PEACE. It's been busy, let me have a couple more days, I'll talk to –

ROY. I said yes, Peace. I took it. I leave at the end of the month.

Pause.

PEACE. Oh.

Scene Five

Saturday.

PEACE *and* ROY *sit as* FAVOUR *busies herself around them.* FAVOUR *is in a good mood.*

FAVOUR. I feel better today.

ROY. You do?

FAVOUR. Much better.

ROY. Well, that's good isn't it, Peace?

PEACE. Yeah. Yes, it's really good.

FAVOUR. We can put that boy behind us. When does he go back?

PEACE. I don't / know –

ROY. This evening.

Pause. FAVOUR *looks at* ROY, *then back at* PEACE. *She paints on a smile.*

FAVOUR. It's a shame, it would have been nice for you to have a relationship with the boy.

PEACE. Yeah.

FAVOUR. What is 'yeah'? Yes, Mummy.

PEACE. Yes, Mummy.

FAVOUR. I don't enjoy being right all the time. I don't enjoy people letting you down.

PEACE. No, Mummy.

FAVOUR. It's a shame. But it's good.

Pause.

ROY. Seeing as you're feeling better –

PEACE. Not now.

FAVOUR. Is something wrong?

PEACE. No.

ROY. Nothing's wrong, we just thought it might be a good time to talk.

PEACE. Roy.

ROY. You said.

FAVOUR. What is it?

PEACE. Nothing.

ROY. Nothing?

PEACE. Well I don't... I don't know yet.

FAVOUR. What is going on? Peace? What do you both keep whispering about?

PEACE *looks helplessly at* ROY *and shakes her head.*

Well speak Roy, you clearly want to.

Pause.

ROY. I have been offered a job abroad and I'm taking it.

FAVOUR. Okay…

FAVOUR *looks at* PEACE *who turns her head away quickly.* FAVOUR *returns her focus to* ROY.

FAVOUR. You are leaving?

ROY. For a year.

FAVOUR. A year?

ROY. Maybe more, but for now. Yeah.

FAVOUR. Okay. Okay. Well enjoy yourself, Roy. Or is there anything else?

ROY. I'd like Peace to come with me.

FAVOUR. Yes of course you would. Has Peace said she wants to go with you?

ROY. We have discussed it.

FAVOUR. And?

ROY. And we wanted to let you know.

FAVOUR. That means no, Roy. No, she doesn't want to go.

ROY. I'm not sure it does, actually.

FAVOUR. And she does not want your feelings to be hurt.

ROY. You're talking for her again, Favour.

FAVOUR. Well it's the truth. Look at her.

Pause. PEACE *and* ROY *look at each other.* ROY *waits for her to speak.*

Roy if you are hoping this ambush of yours will somehow end with you and my daughter taking off around the world –

hear me – it won't. I say that out of kindness, because she is not going to say it.

PEACE *looks away.* ROY *nods.*

I think I will cook for us all tonight eh? Something tasty.

FAVOUR *starts looking through the kitchen cupboards.*

ROY. If she wanted to though, would you let her?

FAVOUR. It is not up to me.

ROY. But if it was? If it was up to you Favour, would you let her go?

FAVOUR *stops.*

FAVOUR. I just want my daughter to be happy. I suggest you let this one go Roy. You may have to drive to the shops and collect extra ingredients.

PEACE. I might want to.

FAVOUR. Sorry?

PEACE. I might… want to go, with Roy.

Pause. ROY *and* FAVOUR *look at* PEACE.

FAVOUR. You?

PEACE. Yes.

FAVOUR. You can't.

ROY. Why not?

FAVOUR. You can't fly.

ROY. Well, she's never flown. There's a difference.

PEACE. I might like it.

FAVOUR. You won't. What are you even thinking? You have a life here, a home here and your friends.

PEACE. I don't… well it's just I don't like my job and I don't have that many friends, not that I couldn't leave. I don't have much of a life here.

FAVOUR. That's not true.

PEACE. And I always wanted –

FAVOUR. You don't want to leave. If you wanted to, you
wouldn't have agreed I should live here for the next year.

Slight pause.

ROY. Excuse me??

FAVOUR. My daughter has been planning to talk to you. She
said it makes more sense if I move in with you both.

ROY. You said what?!

PEACE. *Mum* pl– Babe, no – Mum and I spoke and she said
that maybe – maybe –

FAVOUR. You were going to talk to him in a few days,
daughter.

PEACE *doesn't know what to do.*

ROY. Is this a joke? You had me waiting around to see if you
would move to another country with me at the same you told
your mother she could move into my house?!

PEACE. You said it was our house.

ROY. IT'S MY HOUSE. NOTHING IS OURS PEACE,
NOTHING IS OURS WHILST SHE'S HERE!

Beat.

I can't live like this any more –

FAVOUR. You do not speak to my daughter in that tone.

ROY. Favour, I am begging you just stop –

PEACE. Can you give us a moment?

ROY. Who?

PEACE. You. Can you give me and my mum some time to talk.

ROY. No.

PEACE. I just want –

ROY. No, Peace.

PEACE. Roy please listen to me. Please.

> ROY *looks at* PEACE.

I just need –

> ROY *exits. He has had enough.*

FAVOUR. That boy has a temper.

PEACE. Why did you do that?

FAVOUR. I was helping. Clearly you don't want to go.

PEACE. But I just told you I might want to go. You said you
wanted me to be happy, this might make us happier.

FAVOUR. Well it is not the right time, daughter. I spoke to
estate agents. I told them I wanted to put the house on the
market.

PEACE. When?

FAVOUR. Days ago.

> *Pause.*

PEACE. Did you really do that Mum?

FAVOUR. Yes Peace.

> PEACE *doesn't believe her, but she can't say that.*

PEACE. I still might want to go.

FAVOUR. I don't understand why you're acting so strange,
daughter. Ever since your father passed, you act so strange.
I don't recognise the things that you do. You don't want to be
anywhere else. You like being here.

PEACE. It's just for a year. I can go for a year.

FAVOUR. You don't want to.

PEACE. Mum please stop telling me what I want. Roy's right,
you can't just put words in my mouth.

FAVOUR. I have to when you don't sound like yourself!

That Roy. That Roy doesn't like me. I try so hard but he
doesn't like me. He hates me.

PEACE. No he doesn't.

FAVOUR. He battles me.

PEACE. You are awful to him.

FAVOUR. No it's him. It's them.

PEACE. You don't share, you have to share me –

FAVOUR. He wars against me. You can't see it but I can. He is trying to take you away and you're mine. It was him wasn't it, he made you invite that boy here?

PEACE. This has nothing to do with Bolu.

FAVOUR. Of course it does. Don't you see, they have been conspiring. And you let them confuse you. If you leave it'll be worse. If you leave you will wonder.

PEACE. Wonder? Wonder about what – ?

FAVOUR. Let me come with you?

PEACE. What?

FAVOUR. I want you to carry me around wherever you go and tell people you belong with me.

Beat.

I'm sorry. I'm sorry. I'm not making sense. I don't feel well. I have a migraine. Can you get me some water, can you help me?

Pause. PEACE *gets her mum some water.*

That's better. That's better. I just… I have to keep you with me, I have to keep you safe. It's what I was born do. It's all I want to do.

Pause.

PEACE. Mum… Why didn't you have any more kids?

The song echoes faintly.

Scene Six

Later that day.

PEACE *and* ROY *are in the living room.* PEACE *is fragile.*
ROY *is weary.*

PEACE. I'm… I'm really sorry –

ROY. Please don't, Peace. Not if nothing's gonna… I'm a bit
over you being perpetually sorry to be honest.

PEACE. Right. Yeah. Same.

Pause.

I never wanted my mum to move in here. I just didn't know
how to say no to her.

ROY. Like you didn't know how to say no to me?

PEACE *shakes her head. She looks at* ROY.

PEACE. That's different.

Pause.

It's hard for you isn't it, being with me?

ROY *looks away.*

Roy?

ROY. No.

PEACE. Don't lie, babe. Answer me honestly, if you answer
honestly I promise you I'll do the same. Okay? You find it
difficult?

ROY. Sometimes.

PEACE. Sometimes?

ROY. Yes.

PEACE. It must have been easier when we weren't together.

ROY. It wasn't.

PEACE. Other people you dated then – they were probably easier –

ROY. I don't want to talk about what happened when we broke up. It doesn't matter –

PEACE. I just...

Why are you still here Roy?

ROY *doesn't say anything.*

Why are you with me?

ROY. Why are you with *me*?

PEACE. Because... You. You are genuinely good. Because you make me feel safe. Because I love you. And when you look at me, it's like you've been waiting for me – Like there's something special about me, when I know that I am ordinary.

ROY. Don't –

PEACE. So why me?

ROY. I love you Peace.

Pause.

PEACE. Do you think maybe you took the job to get out of this – away from me?

ROY. No. It's the opposite, I took the job because I want to be somewhere new and start fresh. And I want that for you too.

PEACE. But I don't want to go anywhere. I don't want to go anywhere. I don't like it. I don't like flying – I don't like small spaces – I don't like the dark – I don't enjoy new experiences. I feel better when I'm in places that I know.

ROY. You have to let that go –

PEACE. I don't understand why you expect so much from me.

ROY. You have to let that shit go Peace. It was just a box. It wasn't real life. They were games. Figure out what you actually think.

Pause.

PEACE. I think she's right. I think you are trying to take me away from her.

ROY. Yeah she is. But it's not in a bad way – Not in a controlling way. I just... every part of me hopes that with distance you'll have some perspective.

I'm hoping that if you have space, you'll start asking some questions about yourself.

PEACE. And if I won't the ask questions, will you leave me?

ROY *doesn't answer.*

You could. You could go. I wouldn't be angry. I would understand. I would understand if you found it frustrating to love someone who doesn't have the strength to make her life make sense – Someone who is too afraid... Sometimes Roy, I wish I could get away from myself too. I'm tired. So tired. And I'm not even doing anything.

ROY. But you can.

PEACE *is breaking. Pause.*

You remember that day we met in the park? The day I sprained my ankle?

PEACE. Yeah?

ROY. I faked that.

PEACE. Yeah, I thought so.

ROY. But do you wanna know why?

PEACE. Because you fancied me.

ROY. No. I mean yes – but no. Every day I'd run round that park, I'd be pegging it round and round and you would sit there, gym gear on, looking lost – never quite sure if today was the day you were gonna get up. Whenever I passed your bench I'd slow down, so I could be by you for as long as possible. Then week by week, every lap round that field became me trying to get back to where you sat. You... You were like a song that I couldn't get out of my head. And you

weren't even moving. You are not ordinary. You may think
you're not strong enough to do or change anything, but you
did for me. You just have to be you. You just have to *be*. Run.
Don't run. I'm with you.

Beat. PEACE *believes him. It takes everything for her to ask
the next question.*

PEACE. Has Bolu left yet?

ROY. Not yet.

   PEACE *nods.*

PEACE. I need to speak to him.

Scene Seven

Dark. FAVOUR *sits, her head in her hands.*

FATHER'S VOICE. *Ọjọ kan ṣoṣo la nṣe; ojoojumo loju ntini.*

FAVOUR. *Ọjọ kan ṣoṣo la nṣe; ojoojumo loju ntini.* Yes –
Please shut up my dear.

We never spoke our mother tongue here. Not to each other.
Unless we forgot ourselves. And now in death… when you
lived you were a man who whispered lies and now you are
an ancestor who speaks in fables eh? Now you judge me with
my mother and father and the generations gone before. You
have joined them. The chorus of people I disappointed.

FATHER'S VOICE. She has to hear.

FAVOUR. Why now? You did this too. You started it.

   Beat

But she will forgive you because you are dead.

Scene Eight

Evening.

PEACE *stands alone waiting. She twists the bracelet on her wrist in agitation, thinking.*

ROY *rushes in.*

ROY. I got him here as soon as I could.

> *BOLU enters.*

> I'll – I'll give you both some space. Bolu, when you're finished we'll get you to the airport.

> ROY *looks at* PEACE.

> I'll be upstairs.

> *Roy exits. Then the siblings are left alone. Beat.*

PEACE. Thank you for coming.

BOLU. Where is she?

PEACE. Resting. She doesn't know you're here.

> *Pause.*

> What time's your flight?

BOLU. Soon.

PEACE. Are you going to miss it?

BOLU. Maybe.

PEACE. You might get in trouble for that. Might not be allowed back.

BOLU. I know. Are you ready?

> *Pause.*

> Are you ready to hear *aburo arabinrin*?

PEACE. Yes.

BOLU. Okay. *Bere nkan lowo mi.* Ask me something.

> *Pause.*

PEACE. Why did you take my mum's bracelet?

BOLU. Because it was your mother's bracelet.

PEACE. My...

BOLU. It was our mother's bracelet.

FATHER'S VOICE. I'm sorry.

Pause.

PEACE. Say it.

BOLU. I was three years old when our father left for England. I was young but I remember moments and I've spoken to our neighbours. He used to make the finest tables and chairs in our village, but they say he always dreamed of leaving. He wanted to make furniture for the Queen. Mama, she was not like that. She loved our home. Before he left on a venture to start his business, he made a promise that he was coming back and he made her a crib – yours. She was pregnant with you at the time.

Pause. PEACE *nods. Then starts to cry. She shakes her head back and forth.* BOLU *moves to hold her but* PEACE *holds out her hand.*

PEACE. No. Just tell me. Everything. Please.

BOLU. Half the street were in our house the day I first heard you cry. Not him though. Not yet. You were so loud. You would cry so loud, all the time. So our mama used to sing to soothe you.

PEACE. The song?

BOLU. Yes. A year after you were born, Father came back to us. He came with that woman you now call Mummy. I remember staring at her and wondering who she was, but – she wouldn't look at me. Neither would he, though I stood before him, in my best clothes. Mama started screaming, then you began wailing as I watched, silent. And she – that woman – went to pick you up. Mama tried to stop it but our father wouldn't let her so that woman held you and – you stopped crying. It was all very fast after that. They were leaving with

you and Mama ran out after them, she was calling out –
'Yejide, Yejide'.

PEACE. What's that?

BOLU. Your name.

PEACE. My name? My... They changed my name.

Pause.

BOLU. Yes.

PEACE. When you messaged me, when you found me and you
sent that picture – little you standing next to your mum – I
started crying. Because you had Dad's face, and I had... I'd
never really noticed until I saw that picture. I don't look like
my mum. But I look like yours.

BOLU. You do.

PEACE. They took me and they left you.

BOLU. They stole you. They hid you and they forgot us. I was
never searching for him, Peace. I was searching for you.

PEACE *breaks for a moment.*

PEACE. Does – does she know you've found me?

BOLU. I told Mama a few days after I arrived. But she is
vulnerable. I was taking her bracelet back so she could be
sure. You used to play with that all the time as a baby, I am
surprised they let you keep it.

PEACE. Mum was so annoyed when Dad gave it to me. I
thought it was because she loved it. I didn't know... I didn't,
I didn't – Why didn't she search for me?

BOLU. She never speaks about it. And it is not because she
doesn't care – it is that it hurts too much and she does not
have the strength. I myself used to think it was a dream. But
I could hear you cry in my sleep. For years I've heard it. So
I kept looking until I found you. I wanted to tell you sooner
but you, you were –

PEACE. I wasn't ready, I know I should have –

BOLU. It is not just that. If you had not believed me, or worse, if you had believed but still did not want... I was worried you did not want to be found by us. If not for Roy I might have left without saying anything.

PEACE. Did you tell him?

BOLU. No, no, but I think he could see.

Pause. PEACE *thinks.*

What is it? Ask me.

PEACE. What's she like?

BOLU. Mama? She is warm and generous to a fault. She has a quiet power. She loves deeply. She thinks a lot. She is like you.

PEACE. I don't know what to do, Bolu.

BOLU. You don't have to do anything, you just deserve to know.

PEACE. I should have felt it. I should have – I should have felt it. I –

BOLU. It's going to be okay, sister.

PEACE. You called me 'rootless'.

BOLU. But you're not. You hear? What you are is more than food and language. What you are, Yejide, I cannot take away with words just because I'm angry. If you are going to hold onto anything I've said, hold on to that sister.

ROY *enters. He sees* PEACE.

ROY. She's awake. She's coming down. What do you want to do?

Beat.

FAVOUR *enters. She sees* BOLU.

PEACE. Okay Bolu, let's get you to the airport.

PEACE *starts to get her things.*

FAVOUR. Peace please, let me explain.

PEACE. Let's go –

FAVOUR. It was your father's idea –

PEACE. *Ole to ji kakaki ǫba, o ku i bi ti o fǫn* – That was the one that really scared you. The thief who steals a trumpet will find it difficult to blow without being discovered. I understand now.

FAVOUR. Please, please –

PEACE *heads to the door.*

PEACE. Just make sure you're gone by the time we get back. Bolu, Roy let –

FAVOUR. No wait / just wait

ROY. Are you sure you don't / want to speak to –

PEACE. I'm done –

FAVOUR. Peace, I couldn't have children. I had always wanted to be a mother but I couldn't have children and from the moment I saw you, I knew I had to love you.

PEACE *stops.*

Beat.

ROY. Let me take Bolu.

PEACE. She shouldn't get to explain.

ROY. Not for her. For you. You want to know why, I know you do. Stay.

PEACE *looks at* BOLU.

BOLU. Stay. I'll call when I land. And then you and I will see each other soon. When you visit.

Beat. PEACE *is staying.*

BOLU. Ask her why she changed your name.

BOLU *exits, and just as* ROY *is about to go out after him –*

PEACE. Roy.

ROY *turns to look at* PEACE. *He nods.*

ROY. Me too.

ROY *exits*.

PEACE. Well?

FAVOUR. You have no idea what it was like for me before you and your father.

Your father – He was barely a man when he had Bolu with… Then he came here with his dreams and he met me. You never saw us laugh together, daughter, but we did, in the early days. It wasn't just love. We liked each other. He liked me.

Your father suggested bringing you and Bolu to England. Not me. It was never the plan to separate you, but I knew quickly Bolu would never care for me. So much in his eyes… even as a child. But you, daughter –

PEACE. Why did you change my name?

FAVOUR. You needed me –

PEACE. Why did you change it?

FAVOUR. We had always intended you would know her too but once I had you I –

PEACE. What? Couldn't let go? You only hold on to something that tight when you never should have had it in the first place.

FAVOUR. Please be fair.

PEACE. You think you get to tell me what's fair?! You took me from my mother!

FAVOUR. I am your mother! Wherever you came from, you have always been mine. I have loved you and raised you and dreamed for you.

PEACE. No you have ruined me, you have smothered me and stripped me back, bit by bit.

FAVOUR. That's not true. That's not – You called out for me. You chose me. I have loved you with everything I am – The best way I could – I have suffered and I sacrificed –

PEACE. Well it wasn't enough. Not to make up for what you've done. What you both did. But I can't shout at him. He's dead. And you're all that's left. No wonder he was sorry.

FAVOUR. Peace –

PEACE. Not Peace. I am not Peace, am I? All this time I carried her bracelet, a bit of her with me, and you told me it came from you.

FAVOUR. Because I wanted you to love me.

PEACE. PEACE. Of course I love you!

Beat.

Of course I do. You made me.

That's the point. I have no idea what my life is without all the decisions that you have made.

Pause.

You hid it all. My name, my mother, my brother, my land, and my language. For you. I have lived my whole life – for you.

Beat.

FAVOUR. Are you leaving with Roy?

PEACE. Yes.

FAVOUR *nods*.

FAVOUR. I always imagined as much.

Pause.

FAVOUR. What will you do? When you go? I know you do not have to tell me but…

PEACE. Something new, I think.

Mountains and deserts and rivers.

FAVOUR *nods*.

Beat.

FAVOUR. It means 'image of the mother'. Your name. That is why we changed it.

Not that you responded to it at first... Always my clever girl.

Darling, don't just do something new – you go and be something different.

Yejide.

When the name is said, the drums begin. FAVOUR *winces at the sound then breathes – letting go.*

PEACE. What is that?

For the very first time – PEACE *can hear it too. She looks at* FAVOUR.

Can you hear that?

FAVOUR. All the time. It's for you.

PEACE. But, that's...

FAVOUR. Everything.

Everything. The drums, and the song, and the FATHER'S VOICE. *And many voices. And the castle, and birds, and her mother singing and her father's fables on repeat. The room gloriously shakes with the sound of it.*

FATHER'S VOICE. Yejide.

PEACE. That's –

FAVOUR. They have been calling you.

FATHER'S VOICE. Okay okay okay. Look! It has come! The time has come!

FAVOUR *looks at her daughter, a whisper of a smile on her face.*

FAVOUR. Fly.

FATHER'S VOICE. She will fly now. O she will fly! Look! Look!

PEACE/YEJIDE. Wo.

The drums ring out, and the song calls. The world around PEACE *fades until finally, it's just her – a beacon.*

The End.

Author's Note

In 2020, when the world felt a bit bleak – this story was my song, my form of resistance and the embodiment of all my hopes for the displaced and othered. May we fly, knowing that we are loved, carrying home within us and believing that the *many* who came before us are cheering us on.

F. O.

Thank You

A whole debut. Mad.

Thank you to my family. My tribe. Mum and Dad, you taught me how to be both warrior and dreamer with your resilient strength and belief in the impossible. To my husband Paul. You read every draft, hashed out every idea and answered every worry with – 'What do you need?' My siblings (we don't do in-laws), we know what it is. Wherever I am – we are. Wherever you are – I am.

Thank you to all who worked tirelessly at the Bush. Titilola – you didn't just give this play your hours and weekends, you gave it your passion and your understanding. Lynette and Daniel – thank you for your wisdom, the beautiful check-ins, the joy you both bring into any space and for giving this play its first home.

My writing agent, Jenn: Thank you for all your work and encouragement and for always being there at the end of the phone.

The first readers of this play – Paul, Kenneth, Hollie – every note and observation kept me investigating this story. I'm truly grateful. Thank you to Anjana who kept saying, 'Send it to the Bush, trust me', and to J. Rwothomack – I have not forgotten your words.

And finally – I am so grateful to the people whose words have stimulated my soul and my mind. The friends who consistently reminded me that my voice matters and affirmed me in the face of silence. Named or not – I love you all.

F. O.

104

Glossary

Yoruba	Appropriate Translation
Iyawo mi	My wife.
Wo!	Look!
Yepa!	An exclamation of surprise or shock.
Odẹru ba mi!	You scared me!
Kólòlò	Stammer
Eni to ba mọ ọwọ ararẹ kó nitẹ	If one is mindful of their image, they cannot be disgraced.
Sọ nkan fun mi	Tell me something
Bèrè nkán lọwọ mi	Ask me something
Ẹ´gbọn mi	Brother
Afẹfẹ ko ṣee gbe. Afẹfẹ ko ṣee gbe	The wind it is impossible to carry. It is impossible to carry.
Ole to ji kakaki ọba, o ku i bi ti o fọn	The thief who steals the king's horn, can not blow it without being discovered.
Ilé kì ì jó kí oorun kun ojú	A house could not be burning and we will be sleeping.
Ile ọba t'o jo, ẹwa lo busi	When the king's palace burns down, the re-built palace is even more beautiful.
Ohun ti ájá ri to fi ngbó ko to eyi ti aguntan-an fi nṣeran wo.	What a dog sees and barks at is nothing compared to what the sheep ponders in silence.
Tẹ jẹjẹ	Take it easy/slowly
Ko tiya	Not yet

Mama mi mọ nipa ẹ	My mama knows about it
Jẹ kin ba wọn sọrọ	Let me have a word with them
Iyẹn ti pọ ju	That's too much
Ma pe e pada	I'll call you back
Aburo arabinrin	Sister
Akì í dáké ká ṣìwí; a kì í wò sùn-ùn ká dáràn.	Silence is golden. If you don't get involved, there is no blame.
Ọjọ́ kan là ḿbàjé, ọjọ́ gbogbo lara ńtini.	Only one day brings disgrace to a person; the shame is felt everyday.
	Alternative translation: Reputation spoils in one day – good impression last.
Ọmọ ale	Bastard
Ajẹ ni o.	You are a witch.
Ọjọ kan ṣoṣo la nṣe; ojoojumo loju ntini.	Only one day brings disgrace to a person; the shame is felt everyday.
Yejide	Peace's true name which means 'Image of the Mother'
	Note: A child is usually called 'Yejide' when their mother has died, as if their mother has come back to Earth in their body. Though Peace's mother is alive, the choice of her true name is intentional. A big part of her mother died the day Peace/Yejide was stolen.

A Nick Hern Book

My Father's Fable first published in Great Britain as a paperback original in 2024 by Nick Hern Books Limited, The Glasshouse, 49a Goldhawk Road, London W12 8QP, in association with the Bush Theatre, London

My Father's Fable copyright © 2024 Faith Omole
'Black Crowned Crane' lyrics copyright © 2024 Faith Omole

Faith Omole has asserted her right to be identified as the author of this work

Cover photograph by peeterv via iStock

Designed and typeset by Nick Hern Books, London
Printed in Great Britain by Mimeo Ltd, Huntingdon, Cambridgeshire PE29 6XX

A CIP catalogue record for this book is available from the British Library

ISBN 978 1 83904 372 7

www.nickhernbooks.co.uk/environmental-policy